Piers Compton

THE BROKEN CROSS
The Hidden Hand in the Vatican

Piers Compton

Piers Compton (1901-1986) was a Catholic priest, journalist, and author. He served as Literary Editor of *The Universe* and wrote books, including *Broken Cross*, which criticized changes in the Catholic Church after the Second Vatican Council.

The Broken Cross — The Hidden Hand in the Vatican

First published in Great Britain in 1983

Published by
Omnia Veritas Limited

OMNIA VERITAS®

www.omnia-veritas.com

© Omnia Veritas Ltd - 2025

All rights reserved. No part of this publication may be reproduced by any means without the prior permission of the publisher. The intellectual property code prohibits copies or reproductions for collective use. Any representation or reproduction in whole or in part by any means whatsoever, without the consent of the publisher, the author or their successors, is unlawful and constitutes an infringement punishable by articles of the Code of Intellectual Property.

PART ONE ... 11
2. ... 13
3. ... 15
4. ... 17
5. ... 24
6. ... 27
7. ... 30
8. ... 37
9. ... 42

PART TWO ... 45
2. ... 47
3. ... 56
4. ... 59
5. ... 62

PART THREE ... 65
2. ... 70
3. ... 73
4. ... 76
5. ... 78
6. ... 84
7. ... 89
8. ... 92

PART FOUR ... 95
2. ... 100
3. ... 102

PART FIVE ... 106
2. ... 111

PART SIX ... 119
2. ... 122
3. ... 128

PART SEVEN ... 131
2. ... 138

PART EIGHT ... 140
2. ... 143
3. ... 151
4. ... 154
5. ... 156

PART NINE ... 157
2. ... 160
3. ... 166

PART TEN ... 181
2. ... 185
3. ... 188
4. ... 194

PART ELEVEN ... 195
PART TWELVE ... 201

2	205
PART THIRTEEN	**206**
2	209
3	212
4	220
PART FOURTEEN	**221**
2	229
3	232
APPENDIX	234
The strange death of Roberto Calvi	*234*
FINALE	238
BIBLIOGRAPHY	241
OTHER TITLES	245

Part One

What remains when Rome perishes?
When Rome falls, the world.
Virgil. Byron.

Its claims were monstrous. They passed beyond human reckoning. For it claimed to be the one divine and authoritative voice on earth; and it taught, gave judgment, and asserted, always in the same valid tone, confident that its message would outlive the transitory phenomena of doubt, change, and contradiction. It stood secure, an edifice of truth behind the ramparts of truth which defied the many and various attacks launched by its enemies. For it claimed a strength that was not of itself, a life-force and vigour imparted by a power that could not be found elsewhere; and because it could not be likened to any earthly thing it provoked fear, bewilderment, mockery, even hate.

But through the centuries it never wavered; never abandoned one item of its stupendous inheritance; never allowed the smallest rent to appear in its much derided mantle of intolerance. It inspired devotion and admiration even in those who scorned its mental discipline. It rose above conjecture, likelihood, probability; for the Word by which it had been founded was also its guarantee of permanence. It provided the one answer to the immemorial question — what is truth?

One of our essayists told,[1] as many of our schoolboys used to know, of its place in history; how it saw the beginning, as it was likely to see the end, of our worldly systems; and how, in time to come, a broken arch of London Bridge might furnish a foothold from which a traveller 'could sketch the ruins of St. Paul's.'

But it would still stand monumental, unique, presenting as it did the symbols of endurance in this life and admission to an eternity beyond — a Rock and a Key.

It was the Catholic Church.

But now, as even those of irreligious mind have come to realise, all that has changed. The Church has dropped its guard, surrendered its prerogatives, abandoned its fortifications; and it will be the purpose of these pages to examine how and why the transformation, hitherto regarded by its adherents — and even by some of its unfriendly critics — as impossible, could have happened.

---

[1] Lord Macaulay on von Ranke's *Political History of the Popes*, in 1840.

2.

What follows is written, of set purpose, from the viewpoint of a traditional and still practising Catholic. The sentiments expressed figure here in order to emphasise the heresies, novelties, and profanities that, in the name of reformed or 'updated' religion, have left the Church in tatters throughout the world.

There is a feeling abroad that our civilisation is in deadly peril. It is a recent awareness, wholly distinct from the old evangelical fears that the world, in keeping with some Biblical prophecy, is coming to an end; fears that have lost much of their former simplicity, and have become more real, since the threat of nuclear war. But the end of our civilisation has more sinister implications than has the actual destruction of a planet, whether that be brought about by an 'act of God' or by a frenzy of total madness on the part of man.

For civilisation declines when reason is turned upside down, when the mean and the base, the ugly and corrupt, are made to appear the norms of social and cultural expressions; or, to bring it nearer to the terms of our argument, when evil, under a variety of masks, takes the place of good.

We of this generation, according to our age and temperament, have become the willing, unconscious, or resentful victims of such a convulsion. Hence the air of futility that clings about us, a feeling that man has lost faith in himself and in existence as a whole.

It is true, of course, that every age has suffered the setbacks of war, revolution, and natural disasters. But never before has man been left without guide or compass, without the assurance conveyed by the pressure of a hand in which he trusted. He is, in all too many instances, a separate being, divorced from reality, without the consolation of worthwhile art or background of tradition; and, most fatal of all as the orthodox would say, without religion.

Now it used to be an accepted part of the Catholic outlook that the Church created our civilisation, with the ethical standards, and the great body of revelation, on which man's attitude and destiny depend.

It follows therefore, once that proposition has been accepted, that any falling off on the part of the Church must be reflected by a similar decline in the civilisation it fostered; and such a decline, as evidenced by the moral and cultural expressions of our time, is everywhere visible.

So it is that the mere mention of religion calls forth an automatic rejection on the part of men who have never given a thought to the Church's teaching or practice, but who feel that it should somehow remedy or control the widespread erosion. They feel contempt (and contempt is a more deadly virus than scepticism) for the Church's failure to cope with conditions that call for vital action; for its readiness to go with the stream by not speaking out against, or for even giving encouragement to, subversion; for its preachment of a watered-down version of Humanism in the name of Christian charity; for the way in which, from having been the inflexible enemy of Communism, clerical leaders at the highest level have taken part in what is called 'dialogue' with those who seek, not only the Church's downfall, but the ruin of society as a whole; for the way in which it has surrendered its once proudly defined credo by admitting that there are more gods in heaven and earth than were dreamt of in its Founder's philosophy.

This summary of misgivings brings us back to the question posed at the start of our inquiry — what has caused the changes in the Church?

3.

Any revolution, such as the French and the Russian, must come into headlong collision with two institutions-the monarchy and the Church. The former, however deeply it may be rooted in lineage and sacramental rite, can be totally disposed of by a single blow. But a peoples' religion, however defective it may have become, cannot be so easily suppressed by any force exerted from without.

Monarchy lives by acceptance, custom, and a process of recognition that can be brought to an end by the fall of a knife or the discharge of a rifle. But religion, and especially the Christian, although it may have become discredited and subject to scorn, has so far carried within itself the seeds of resurrection. Time and again. a sentence of death has gone out against it; time and again it has outlived the executioner. That it will continue to do so may be taken for granted, though whether it will survive in its old untrammelled form, with its stature, infallible voice, and stamp of authority, is another matter.

Some will reject that suggestion as unthinkable. Others, while agreeing that the Church has sanctioned a change of emphasis, here and there, will see it as part of the divine plan; and only a few, since it has become a characteristic of our people to reject the mere mention of a conspiracy, will see in it the working out of an age-long and deliberate scheme to destroy the Church from within. Yet there is more proof of every kind for the existence of such a conspiracy than there is for some of the commonly accepted facts of history.

Because of what follows it needs to be repeated that the average British mind does not take kindly to the idea of a 'plot.' The very word savours of a theatrical setting, with heavily cloaked men meeting in a darkened room to plan the destruction of their enemies. But secret scheming, hidden for the most part from the academic as from the public mind, has been the background or driving force of much world history.

The world of politics is bedevilled by cliques working one against another, as becomes evident when we take note of the flaws that occur in official versions of the Gunpowder Plot, the murder of Abraham Lincoln in 1865, that of the Archduke Francis Ferdinand of Austria at Sarajevo in 1914, the drowning of Kitchener in 1916, the shooting of President Kennedy in 1963, and even nearer to our own time, the mysterious end of Pope John Paul I, to be dealt with later in this volume.

4.

The Church has always been the target of anti-religious men who see in its existence a threat to their progress and designs. And I use the word 'always' advisedly, for plotting against the Church occurs as early as the year A.D. 58. in words spoken by St. Paul to the people of Ephesus (and Paul, a trained Pharisee, when it came to warning against subversion knew what he was saying): 'After my departure, grievous wolves shall come in among you, not sparing the flock; and from among your own selves shall issue men speaking perverse things in order to draw away the disciples after them.'

The urge for world domination whether by force of arms, culture, or religion, is as old as history. The earliest records, without considering myth or even legend, give proof of it. Egypt, which first dominated the thought and outlook of the East, was never a purely military State. But a warlike era emerged (we may date it from about 910 B.C.) with 'Assyria the Terrible.' The rise of Babylon, short-lived, was followed by that of Persia, under Cyrus the Great. Then came a name that has never ceased to be synonymous with that of a vast empire and lordship of the known world, Rome. But all such powers, apart from being concerned with territorial gain, aimed also at imposing some political or social creed, the overthrowing of one standard belief and the elevation of another, a process that the ancients used to associate with the influence of the gods.

The spread of the Arian heresy, that split Christendom throughout the fourth century, becomes a landmark. It involved all the symptoms of revolution, anarchy, treachery, and intrigue. But the underlying cause was not political. Its mainspring was religious, even theological, since it turned upon a phrase coined by Arius, the Alexandrian priest whose name was given to the movement: 'There must have been a time when Christ was not.'

That denigration of the divine being and nature of Christ, if carried to its logical conclusion, would have rendered the world that was centred on Rome to a negative state in which Europe, as we know it, would have had no future. But Rome survived, as a place of reverence for some, as a target for others; and what we now look back upon as the medieval world was filled with repercussions of the same struggle.

With the consolidation of Rome as a Papal power the objective became a more definite reality, with its purpose never in doubt and always the same, whatever temporal or domestic interpretation was placed upon it.

For the eyes of men, whether in France, Italy or Spain, England or Germany, were on Peter's Chair, an object of controversy that has proved more potent than gold in bearing on the mind.

That was the situation in Rome during the first quarter of the twelfth century, when two rival families, the Pierleoni and the Frangipani, were angling for power. Both were rich, the Pierleoni immensely so; neither was over-scrupulous; and when the Pope, Callistus II, died in 1124, both families put up a candidate for the Papal throne. The Pierleoni's man, Anacletus, was 'not thought well of, even by his friends.' But he managed to outvote his rival who was backed by the Frangipani.

Anacletus's reign was short and unpopular, but he clung perilously to power until his death in 1138, when he was declared anti-pope in favour of Innocent II. So it came about that an organised clique, if only briefly, took over the Vatican where they installed 'their man', a looked-for consummation that figured in the minds of international plotters until, in our own time, it came to be realised.

It is a curious fact that man will suffer more readily for ideas, however crude, than he will for positive causes that affect his way of life; and when the perennial heresy of Gnosticism raised its head at the little town of Albi, in southern France, at the start of the thirteenth century, men flocked to it as once they had to join a crusade. But this time its principles were more extreme than those of any Christian warrior. Matter was declared to be evil; so death, which meant the ending of matter, became more desirable than life. Suicide, often brought about by men starving themselves, and their families, was a privilege and a blessing; and the very foundations of the Church, with the Papal throne, were shaken as hundreds of clergy, with as many nuns, came out on the side that had more political and philosophic undertones than appear in many stories of the period.

It was a life and death struggle in which the Church, under Pope Innocent III, reacted violently by setting up the Inquisition. Its purpose was to examine Albigensians who, purporting to be orthodox, had entered the Church, and occupied some of its most exalted places in order to undermine authority and set up, in every sphere, a system of common ownership. The capture of the Papacy was, of course, their main objective, although most histories of the time are more concerned with the fate of those who failed to recite the 'Our Father' correctly before their questioners.

The violence and cruelty of the war that set in has left a permanent mark on history. The terms Albigensian and Inquisition are often employed as useful steps to an argument. Few realise the true significance of the struggle which left the Papal throne still secure, so far invulnerable, but always, under several guises and from any part of Europe, the object of attack.

From this time on that attack was more concentrated. It gathered strength. In 1482, at Strasbourg, it gained a new intensity as the enemies of the Pope declared their intention of waging war against him. A document dated 1535, and known as the Charter of Cologne, is evidence of the same hostility, and equally violent. Echoes of the Albigensian campaign, still insisting that non-existence was preferable to what its followers called the Satanic ordering of earthly life, lingered on in a traditionally orthodox and never thickly populated country like Portugal, where the continued activity of the Inquisition was such that, among the dozens of those sentenced to death between the years 1619 and 1627, were fifty-nine priests and nuns.

During the latter years of the eighteenth century a young man was pacing the streets of Ingolstadt, Bavaria, with hatred in his heart and a fixed determination in his mind. His hatred was directed against the Jesuits, the religious Society which had trained him and made him a Professor of Canon Law at the local university, a Society which has, incidentally, always been a successful breeding ground for nearly every type of saint and assassin.

His determination, shared at one time or another by many serious-minded young men, but all too often without dedication, was to work for the overthrow of Church and State. But his determination had roots, and Adam Weishaupt (for that was his name), was now reaping the benefit of the Society he had come to despise.

For the spirit of the first Jesuit, Ignatius Loyola, had come down to even the apostates among his followers. Ignatius had been, as was then not uncommon in his native Spain, a gentleman soldier. He had stood fire, and known the shock of enemy metal. And Adam Weishaupt could view the prospect before him with a military mind. He had thrust, and vision. He knew the value of surprise, which is grounded in secrecy. And he was single-minded. All around him was strife of some sort, and contradiction. He would blend mankind into one whole, eliminate tradition, which differs from people to people, and suppress dogma, which invites more untruths than the one it sets out to establish.

Not for the first time, and certainly not for the last, a man set himself apart from his fellows in the name of universal brotherhood. The ideal state that Weishaupt had in mind was, of course, founded on the impossible dream of human perfection; hence his first followers went by the arrogantly priggish name of Perfectibilists.

But it soon became clear that moral impeccability was less conducive to his ends than mental enlightenment; and on the 1st day of May, 1776, the secret society that was to profoundly affect much subsequent history came into existence as the Illuminati. The date and certain of its implications are noteworthy. For on May the 1st the great Celtic pagan festival of Beltane was celebrated on hills that, wherever possible, were pyramidal in shape.

The Illuminati had by then, according to a plan they had made known in Munich in the previous year, decided on a most ambitious line of conduct. It would form and control public opinion. It would amalgamate religions by dissolving all the differences of belief and ritual that had kept them apart; and it would take over the Papacy and place an agent of its own in the Chair of Peter.

A further project was to bring down the French monarchy, which had long been a powerful influence, second only to the Papacy, in maintaining the existing European order. To that end a most efficient go-between was found in the person of one Joseph Balsamo, better known as Cagliostro, one of the world's most agile performers on the make-believe stage.

He was backed financially, as are most if not all anarchistic leaders, by a group of bankers under the House of Rothschild. It was under their direction that the long range and world-wide plans of the Illuminati were drawn up.

Cagliostro's excursions in the realm of the occult have earned him a variety of epithets. He was charlatan, astrologer, the possessor of the secret of eternal youth and of the great universal medicine. But his claim to be possessed of an other-world influence may not have been wholly false. For after having survived the tests that made him a full blooded Illuminatus (the ceremony took place at night, in an underground vault near Frankfurt) he journeyed from country to country, in a black varnished coach that was decorated with magic symbols, imposing his arts upon the most influential circles, yet always with an eye on the French Court where he soon picked on Marie Antoinette as its most valuable and susceptible member.

How he finally over-reached himself, in perpetrating the swindle of the diamond necklace,[2] is part of the preparatory process that led to the outbreak of the French Revolution. He died most miserably in Rome, but not without leaving a reputation that still poses questions, and which is typical of the formidable effects derived from contact with the Illuminati.

As part of the secrecy that masked its strength, and also perhaps from a juvenile wish to claim classical connections, the leaders of the Society adopted classical names, mostly from Greek or Roman myth and history. Adam Weishaupt became Spartacus, the name of the Thracian slave who led a revolt against Rome. His second-in-command, Baron Knigge, chose Philo, after the neo-Platonic philosopher. The uncouth sounding Franz Zwackh elected to be Cato, the Roman statesman. The Marquis Costanzo (for the Illuminati made free with titles) became Diomedes, one of the Greek leaders in the Trojan War; while a certain Francis Mary Arouet, undersized, warped, and wizened, coined a name for himself that was destined to sound through the popular consciousness like a miniature thunder-clap — Voltaire.

It is a common enough procedure for the casual reader to glance at, or even study, the names of those who directed the anti-Bourbon fury that swept over Paris, and most of France, without realising that much of it stemmed from the Illuminati, whose members were prominent in the short-lived committees and assemblies spawned by the Revolution.

Mirabeau and Danton were two of its nearly gigantic figures. Dapper little Robespierre supplied the consistency, and the tortuous Fouche the self-preserving cunning, of ice-cold brains. Talleyrand limped his way over obstacles that proved fatal to more active men. Camille Desmoulins exhibited an adolescent faith in his fellows. Marshals Murat, Massena, Bernadotte, and Soult followed the direction of Napoleon's bicorne hat and drove

---

[2] A complicated affair involving a Cardinal's thwarted passion, impersonation, and forged letters. Well treated by Hilaire Belloc in his book on *Marie Antoinette*, who was dragged down by the scandal.

his enemies from field after field. Kellermann, as heavy as his name, remained firmly booted and spurred, unlike Lafayette, who could change his royal uniform for the garb of a republican or a diplomat. All these were Illuminati. Some worked with open eyes, actual accomplices. Others, like Desmoulins, were enthusiasts or dupes.

Their influence did not die with them. It was passed on, long after the guillotine had gone out of common use, and could be recognised as the power behind the Directory. It lessened throughout the Consulate, but came back reinforced when Louis XVIII was hoisted on to the throne after Waterloo, and it sparked off the Revolution of 1830, which signalled the end of the Bourbons whom the Illuminati had long before marked down for ruin.

5.

The sinister designs of Weishaupt and his Society had been made known to the Bavarian Government, as the result of a thunderstorm, in 1785.

A former priest and henchman of Weishaupt, named Joseph Lanz, had been out in the storm to deliver a message, when he was struck by lightning and killed. His body was taken to the chapel of a Benedictine convent where a nun, who prepared him for burial, found documents sewn into his clothing. Their importance, it soon became clear, reached far beyond the convent, and they were passed to the authorities who rubbed their eyes on seeing they outlined a plot for overthrowing Church and State. Weishaupt was banished from Bavaria, but he promptly fell on his feet again by being protected and pensioned by the Prince of Saxe-Gotha.

By the time of Weishaupt's death in 1830 the hand of his Society could be detected in countries other than France, though its workings were sometimes indistinguishable from those of the more politically minded Italian movement, the Carbonari (charcoal burners). That Society had been founded by Maghella in Naples at the time of the former Marshal Murat, who had been created King of Naples by Napoleon. Its declared object was to drive out foreigners and to set up a republican constitution.

The peculiar strength of such bodies has always been their secrecy, and this was in no way impugned by the signs and symbols they adopted. Sometimes they had an affected occult significance, that was meant to be impressive, and this often led them to introduce merely puerile, absurd, or even unpleasant rites of initiation. There was, for instance, one Illuminati circle that persuaded candidates to enter a bath of water — persuaded, that is, by pulling them towards the bath by means of a piece of string that was tied to their genitals. And it was this perverted sexual obsession that made some of Weishaupt's disciples undergo self-castration.

But some rites and symbols derived an undeniable significance from what is generally called Black Magic, or from the invocation of a Satanic power whose potency runs like a sinister streak through pages of Biblical, legendary, and historically verified writing.

'By symbols,' said Thomas Carlyle in *Sartor Resartus*, 'is man guided and commanded, made happy, made wretched. He everywhere finds himself surrounded with symbols, recognised as such or not recognised.'

The Illuminati made use of a shape that was probably old when Egypt reached its peak, that of a pyramid, or triangle, which has long been known to initiates as a sign of mystic or solar faith. At the top of that pyramid, or sometimes at its base, was, and in fact still is, the image of a separate human Eye, which has been variously referred to as the open eye of Lucifer, the morning star, or the eternal watcher of the world and the human scene.

The pyramid was one of the symbols that represented the unknown and nameless deity in pre-Christian cults. Centuries later it was resurrected as a symbol of the destruction of the Catholic Church; and when the first phase of that destruction had been brought about, as we shall see, by those who had infiltrated and since occupied, some of the highest places in the Church, they reproduced it as a sign of their success.

It overlooked the crowds who gathered for the Philadelphia Eucharistic Congress in 1976. It was taken up by the Jesuits who edited the Society's year book; and it appeared on a series of Vatican stamps issued in 1978.

The Eye, which can be traced back to the Babylonian moon-worshippers, or astrologers, came to represent the Egyptian trinity of Osiris, the sun; Isis, the moon goddess; and their child, Horus. Isis also appeared in Athens, Rome, Sicily, and other centres of antiquity under a variety of names including Venus, Minerva, Diana, Cybele, Ceres, Proserpine, and Bellona. The

Eye came to figure among the mystic solar symbols of Jove, Baal, and Apollo.

There was nothing empty or childish in the Society's claim that its members, as evidenced by the Eye, were under constant surveillance. 'It is understood,' so ran a dictum of the Society, 'that anyone who reveals our secrets, either voluntarily or involuntarily, signs his own death warrant.'

And those words have been borne out, time and again. One of the first to give an instance of this was a Frenchman, named Lescure, whose son had played a briefly prominent part in the Revolution. Lescure senior was admitted to the cult of the Eye and the pyramid. But he soon repented, refused to attend their gatherings, was looked upon as a possible danger to his erstwhile brethren, and died suddenly of poison. In his last lucid moments he blamed 'that impious horde of the Illuminati' for his death.

6.

Mention has already been made of the Carbonari, the Supreme Directory of which, known as the *Alta Vendita*,[3] became a kind of nucleus for all the secret societies spread through Italy. In organization and intention it was much the same as the Illuminati. Its leaders adopted a similar brand of whimsical appellations (such as Little Tiger, Nubius, Vindex, Minos), and it exhibited the same unremitting hostility towards Church and State.

This was clearly outlined in a set of *Permanent Instructions*, or Code of Rules, which appeared in Italy in 1818. It was written by Nubius and was addressed to a fellow conspirator called Volpi, with suggested guide lines and news of what had so far been accomplished.

Nubius, who appears to have been a man of rank in Rome, starts with a modest appraisal of the not insignificant task that had been entrusted to him. 'As I told you before, I have been appointed to demoralise the education of the youth of the Church.' But he was not unaware of the most difficult obstacle he would have to encounter. One great problem remained. 'The Papacy has always exercised a decisive influence over Italy. With the arm, the voice, the pen, of its innumerable bishops, monks, nuns, and faithful of all latitudes, the Pope finds everywhere people who are prepared for sacrifice, and even for martyrdom, friends who would die for him, or sacrifice all for his sake.

'It is a mighty lever, the full power of which few Popes have understood, and which has yet been used but partially....

---

[3] Literally the 'old shop' or the 'old sale.' Secret society meetings were often disguised as auction sales to avert suspicion.

Our final aim is that of Voltaire, and that of the French Revolution — the complete annihilation of Catholicism, and ultimately of Christianity. Were Christianity to survive, even upon the ruins of Rome, it would, a little later on, revive and live.

'Take no notice of those boastful and vainglorious Frenchmen, and thick-headed Germans, and hypochondriacal Englishmen, who think it possible to end Catholicism by an obscene song, or by a contemptible sarcasm. Catholicism has a vitality which survives such attacks with ease. She has seen adversaries more implacable, and more terrible far, and sometimes has taken a malicious pleasure in baptising with holy water the most rabid amongst them.

'Therefore the Papacy has been for seventeen hundred years interwoven with the history of Italy. Italy can neither breathe nor move without the leave of the Supreme Pontiff. With him, she has the hundred arms of Briareus; without him, she is condemned to a lamentable impotency. Such a state of things must not continue. It is necessary to seek a remedy.

'Very well. The remedy is at hand. The Pope, whoever he may be, will never enter into a secret society. It therefore becomes the duty of the secret societies to make the first advance to the Church, and to the Pope, with the object of conquering both. The work for which we gird ourselves is not the work of a day, nor of a month, nor of a year. It may last for many years, perhaps a century. In our ranks the soldier dies, but the work is continued.

'We do not at present intend to gain the Pope to our cause. That which we should await, as the Jews await a Messiah, is a Pope according to our wants. We require a Pope for ourselves, if such a Pope were possible. With such a one we shall march more securely to the storming of the Church, than with all the little books of our French and English brothers. And why?

'Because it were useless to seek with these alone to split the Rock upon which God has built the Church. We should not want the vinegar of Hannibal,[4] nor gunpowder, nor even our arms, if we had but the little finger of the successor of Peter engaged in the plot; that little finger will avail us more for our crusade than all the Urbans and St. Bernards for the crusade of Christianity.

'We trust that we may yet attain this supreme object of our efforts. Little can be done with the old Cardinals and with prelates of decided character. In our magazines, either popular or unpopular, we must find the means to utilise, or ridicule, the power in their hands. A well invented report must be spread with tact amongst good Christian families.

Such a Cardinal, for instance, is a miser; such a prelate is licentious. These things will spread rapidly in the cafes, thence to the squares, and one report is sometimes enough to ruin a man.

'If a prelate arrives in a province from Rome to officiate at some public function, it is necessary at once to become acquainted with his character, his antecedents, his temperament, his defects — especially his defects. Give him a character that must horrify the young people and the women; describe him as cruel, heartless, or bloodthirsty; relate some atrocious transaction which will cause a sensation amongst the people. The foreign newspapers will learn and copy these facts, which they will know how to embellish according to their usual style...'

---

[4] Ancient historians considered that the Alpine passes were too narrow to afford passage to Hannibal's army, with its elephants, and that he must have used hot vinegar to split the rock.

7.

Apart from the earlier indications, the main purpose of the plot, to gain control of the Papacy, had been brought to light in Florence by an opponent of the secret societies named Simonini, who carried the news of their intention to Pius VII.

But the Church could do little more in the way of defence than issue warnings; while the Carbonari, reinforced by the positive declarations uttered by the *Alta Vendita*, pressed home its attacks.

A few years after that document was issued, Little Tiger addressed the Piedmontese group of the society in the following terms: 'Catholicism must be destroyed throughout the whole world. Prowl about the Catholic sheepfold and seize the first lamb that presents itself in the required conditions. Go even to the depths of convents. In a few years the young clergy will have, by the force of events, invaded all the functions. They will govern, administer, and judge.

They will be called upon to choose the Pontiff who will reign; and the Pontiff, like the greater part of his contemporaries, will be necessarily imbued with the principles which we are about to put into circulation.

'It is a little grain of mustard which we will place in the earth, but the sun of justice will develop it to become a great power, and you will see one day what a rich harvest that little seed will produce.'

The policy of infiltration had already been put into effect, and Little Tiger was soon claiming that a new breed of priests, talented young men who were likely to rise high in the hierarchy, had been trained to take over and destroy the Church. And that was no empty boast, since in 1824 he was telling Nubius: 'There are certain members of the clergy, especially in Rome, who have swallowed the bait, hook, line, and sinker.'

The persistence, the thoroughness, and the single-minded purpose of the societies which, then as now, was not to be found outside them, was never in doubt. 'Let the clergy march under your banner in the belief that they march under the banner of the Apostolic Keys. Do not fear to slip into the religious communities, into the very midst of their flock.

Let our agents study with care the personnel of those confraternity men, put them under the pastoral staff of some virtuous priest, well known but credulous and easy to be deceived. Then infiltrate the poison into those chosen hearts; infiltrate it by little doses as if by chance.'

This was soon followed by a confident assessment of the inroads that the societies had already made. 'In Italy, they count among their numbers more than eight hundred priests, among whom are many professors and prelates as well as some Bishops and Cardinals!' It was claimed that many of the Spanish clergy were also involved.

But, as Nubius constantly repeated, all interim victories would be hollow until a Pope who was part of their ultimate design was occupying Peter's Chair. 'When that is accomplished,' he wrote in 1843, 'you will have established a revolution led by the tiara and the pluvial (ceremonial) cape; a revolution brought about with little force, but which will strike a flame in the four corners of the world.'

There was a feeling of change in the air, a change that would extend beyond the boundaries of the Church and transform many facets of existence. Little Tiger summed it up hopefully to Nubius in 1846: 'All feel that the old world is cracking.' And his finger must have been on the pulse of events, for two years later a highly select body of secret initiates who called themselves the League of Twelve Just Men of the Illuminati, financed Karl Marx to write the Communist Manifesto, and within months Europe was rocking with revolution.

But Nubius did not live long enough to sample whatever benefits might have come about. For activated by rumours, whether true or false, that he was letting his tongue wag too freely, the all-seeing Eye was turned in his direction and Nubius succumbed to a dose of poison.

We of this generation have lived through, and are still encountering, the political and religious aftermaths of a struggle whose causes were hidden from those who witnessed its early stages, just as they are from us who are blindly groping a way through its secondary phases. For its perpetrators, and their operations, are masked by secrecy, a secrecy so continuous, and profound, that it cannot be matched elsewhere.

When the French author, Cretineau-Joly, brought the sinister import of the *Alta Vendita* to the notice of Pope Pius IX (1846-78), who allowed his name to be used as a guarantee of its authority, the event, that should have called for a fanfare of silver trumpets, was drowned by the petty whistling of Parliamentary verbiage and cant. And when Adolphe Cremieux, Minister of Justice, as reported in *Les Archives,* Paris, in November 1861, voiced the precept that 'Nationalities must disappear, religion must be suppressed,' the circles that framed such statements saw that they were never diffused as forecasts of a condition that would clamour for widespread acceptance in less than a century.

Again, a reader of *The Times*, in Victorian England, would have noted, perhaps with an insular distaste for everything Latin, the disorders that flared from time to time in Spain, Portugal, Naples, and the Papal States. In seeking an explanation, the word 'dagos' might have suggested itself. But one thing is certain. He would never have thought that the man who master-minded the turmoil was no less a person than Lord Palmerston, who was the Queen's Foreign Secretary between the years 1830-51, Prime Minister in 1855, and again in 1859 until his death in 1865.

For behind those Parliamentary titles, he was known to his fellow-conspirators as Grand Patriarch of the Illuminati, and therefore controller of all the sinister complex of secret societies. Glance at some of their political designs — the achievement of a united Italy under the House of Savoy; the annexation of Papal territory; the reconstitution of a Polish State; the deprivation of Austria, and the consequent rise of the German Empire.

Each of those objectives, irrespective of time, was set down on the Illuminati's agenda. Each has been attained; and Benjamin Disraeli, who knew the whole business of plot and counter-plot, doubtless had Palmerston's machinations in mind when he said, in 1876: 'The Governments of this country have to deal, not only with governments, kings, and ministers, but also with secret societies, elements which must be taken into account, which at the last moment can bring all plans to naught, which have agents everywhere, who incite assassinations and can, if necessary, lead a massacre.'

The leaders of the Italian Revolution, Mazzini, Garibaldi, and Cavour were the servants of the Eye, while such monarchs of the time as Victor Emmanuel II and Napoleon III also came within its radius.

Throughout the remainder of the century the attack on orthodoxy gathered weight. In 1881 the Prime Minister of France, Leon Gambetta, could openly declare; 'Clericalism, that is the enemy.' A more popular orator roared: 'I spit upon the rotting corpse of the Papacy.' And the same year provided ample evidence of the hostility that was ready to break out in the most unexpected parts of the continent. For when the body of Pius IX was being transferred from the Vatican basilica to the church of St. Lawrence — outside-the-Walls, the cortège was attacked by a mob armed with cudgels. Amid their shouted obscenities a street battle developed before the body of the dead Pope could be saved from being flung into the Tiber. The authorities, siding with the rioters, took no action.

So in that way, and by many devious routes, the contests of early Christian times, and of the Middle Ages, were being continued. But now the Church's enemies were shifting their attacks from open warfare to peaceful penetration, which was more in keeping with the spirit of the time.

'What we have undertaken,' proclaimed the Marquis de la Franquerie in the middle of the last century, 'is the corruption of the people by the clergy, and that of the clergy by us, the corruption which leads the way to our digging the Church's grave.'

An even more confident prediction, and on a new note, was made some sixty years later: 'Satan must reign in the Vatican. The Pope will be his slave.' Confirmation of this, and in much the same words was to be given in a revelation received by three illiterate children aged ten, eight, and seven respectively, at the little town of Fatima in Portugal in 1917. It took the shape of a warning that, at that time of day, seemed frankly ridiculous: 'Satan will reign even in the highest places. He will even enter the highest position in the Church.'

Some indication of the prophetic, or carefully planned projects of the secret societies, may be read into a letter addressed to Mazzini, dated April the 15th, 1871, and catalogued in the British Museum Library. At that time wars were conducted on a comparatively small and restricted scale, but this letter, written more than forty years before the first world conflict started, may be interpreted as a forecast of the Second World War, together with more possible hints of a third and still greater catastrophe that is yet to come. Here it is quoted:

'We will unleash the Nihilists and atheists, and we will provoke a formidable social catastrophe which, in all its horror, will show clearly to the nations the effect of absolute atheism, original savagery, and the most bloody turmoil.

'Then everywhere the citizens, obliged to defend themselves against the majority of world revolutionaries, will extinguish the destroyers of civilisations; and the multitude, disillusioned with Christianity, whose deistic spirits will be from that time without compass, anxious for an ideal, but without knowing where to render its adoration, will receive the true light through the universal manifestation of the pure doctrine of Lucifer, brought finally out to the public view, a manifestation which will result from the general revolutionary movement which will follow the destruction of Christianity and atheism, both conquered and exterminated at the same time.'

In the above a term is used that, in the course of these pages, may call for clarification. It needs to be understood that the enemies of the Church were not atheists according to the commonly accepted meaning. They rejected religion as represented by the Christian God whom they refer to as Adonay, a being who has, they say, condemned the human race to a recurring round of suffering and darkness.

But their intelligence calls for the recognition of a god, and they found one in Lucifer, son of the morning and bearer of light, the brightest of the archangels who led the heavenly revolution in a bid to make himself the equal of God.

The highly developed Luciferian creed, until the end of the 1939 war, was directed throughout the world from a centre in Switzerland. Since that time its headquarters have been located in the Harold Pratt Building, New York.

But although such places may be named, the veil of secrecy surrounding the inner circle of world government has never been broken. Nothing else in the world has remained so hidden, so intact; and the existence of such an inner circle was acknowledged by no less a person than Mazzini who, although one of the arch conspirators, was compelled to admit, in a letter written shortly before his death to a Doctor Breidenstine: 'We form an association of brothers in all points of the globe. Yet there is one unseen who can hardly be felt, yet it weighs on us. Whence comes it? Where is it? No one knows, or at least, no one talks. This association is secret even to us, the veterans of secret societies.'

The Voice, the universal brotherhood magazine, first published in England in 1973, later transferred to Somerset West, Cape Province, South Africa, has this to say about it: 'The Elder Brothers of the Race usually move through the world unknown. They seek no recognition, preferring to serve behind the scenes.'

In his often quoted book *1984*, George Orwell refers to this inner party, or universal brotherhood, and how, apart from its secrecy, the fact of its not being an organisation in the usual sense makes it invulnerable. While Sir Winston Churchill, in his study of

Great Contemporaries, says: 'Once the apparatus of power is in the hands of the Brotherhood, all opposition, all contrary opinions, must be extinguished by death.'

And there are enough strange deaths recorded even in these pages to make one pause over that.

8.

The introduction of Satan as a fresh element in the struggle met with less response in heterodox England than it did upon the continent. For there, belief in the positive power of evil, and cases of diabolical possession, were not always regarded as moonshine. What had happened at the Ursuline convent at Louviers, in Normandy, and at another convent (also Ursuline) at Aix-en-Provence, in the region of Marseilles, both in the seventeenth century, could still inspire nervous glances over the shoulder.

At Louviers, young nuns and novices had there attended Black Masses where the Host was consecrated over the private parts of a woman stretched upon the altar. Portions of the Host had then been inserted into those parts. One of the Franciscan friars who served the convent dealt in love philtres made of the sacramental wafer dipped in menstrual blood and that of murdered babies.

At the other convent, a young girl had writhed on the ground, exposing every part of her body, and screaming obscenities relating to sodomy and cannibalism. Other members of the community claimed that their minds and bodies were being tormented by Beelzebub, the demon worshipped by the Philistines, the so-called Lord of the Flies because he appeared dripping sacrificial blood that attracted hordes of flying insects. In both cases the evil influence was traced to Satanically inspired priests, who perished at the stake. Part of the evidence, at the trial of one, was a pact with Satan signed in the priest's blood.

Later in the same century the Abbé Guibourg celebrated the same kind of mock religious rite sometimes with the help of Madame de Montespan, one of the fading mistresses of Louis XIV, who took part in the hope of reviving the King's passion for her. There again the blood of a murdered child, and that of a bat, mingled with the sperm of the officiating priest to boost the sacramental wine.

It was common for the mock celebrant on such occasions to wear a cardinal's robes. Black candles stood on the altar.

The cross was in evidence, but reversed, and there were pictures showing a crucifix being trampled by a goat. A star, a black moon, and a serpent figured in erotic paintings around the walls, and the only name spoken in reverence was that of Lucifer. Initiates frequently received Communion at a properly constituted church, but it was only to carry the Host away in their mouths and then to feed it to animals and mice.

A typical Black Magic centre, or Temple of Satan, was set up in Rome in 1895. A group of interested people, curious to sample its meaning, somehow managed to penetrate a little beyond its threshold, and what they saw was described by one of them, Domenico Margiotta: [5] 'Its lateral walls were hung with magnificent red and black damask draperies.[6] At the further end was a great piece of tapestry upon which was the figure of Satan at whose feet was an altar.

'Here and there were arranged triangles, squares, and other symbolic signs. All around stood gilt chairs. Each of these, in the moulding which cupped its back, had a glass eye, the interior of which was lighted by electricity, while in the middle of the temple stood a curious throne, that of the Great Satanic Pontiff.' Something in the silent atmosphere of the room terrified them, and they left more quickly than they had entered.

With the Illuminati raising its head again, and even as far afield as Russia, there were signs that its influence had penetrated the top level of the Church. It had done so in the person of Cardinal Mariano Rampolla (1843-1913) one of those significant, yet

---

[5] *La Croix du Dauphiné,* 1895.

[6] Colours that are frequently mentioned throughout this book, especially at the initiation of Pope John XXIII.

shadowy and largely unknown figures whose like can be found only in the covertly sinister pages of Vatican history.

A native of Sicily, and a Liberal in outlook, he entered Papal service during the pontificate of Leo XIII, and had been Secretary of Propaganda before becoming Secretary of State.

An Englishman who claimed to have known him, and to have made him acquainted with the occult, was Aleister Crowley, who had been born in the then demulcent town of Leamington in 1875, and who had then passed, by way of Cambridge, to become one of the most controversial figures in the world of mystery. People of intelligence still shake their heads over trying to answer such questions as to whether he was a master of the Black Arts, a dabbler in them, or merely a pretender. Somerset Maugham, who knew him well, gave his opinion that Crowley was a fake, 'but not wholly a fake.'

He was certainly, as shown by his writings, a master of corruption. For what may be most charitably called his spiritual aspirations were tempered by a blatant sensualism. It was through the flesh that his being leapt out to embrace mystery. The images that passed into his mind came out deformed, often with a sexual connotation; and, like others of his kind who wander on the border of the unknown, he found comfort in sheltering behind a variety of fantastic names such as Therion, Count Vladimir Svaroff, Prince Chiva Khan, the Laird of Boleskin, a title that he tried to live up to by wearing a kilt. To his mother he was the Great Beast (from the Apocalypse). Crowley responded by calling her a brainless bigot.

By filing his two canine teeth he made them into fangs, which enabled him to implant a vampire's kiss on the throat or wrist of any woman who was unlucky enough to meet him. He married Rose Kelly, a sister of the painter Sir Gerald, who later became President of the Royal Academy.

She was a weak sub-normal creature, who could evidently overlook his pleasant little way of hanging a mistress upside down by her heels in a wardrobe, just as she could agree with the names he bestowed upon their daughter, I Nuit Ahotoor Hecate Sappho Jezebel Lilith.

Whether or not there was any definite connection between Rampolla and Crowley, the Cardinal's steady rise in the hierarchy offered a solid contrast to Crowley's futile preoccupation with the societies of the Golden Dawn and the Oriental Templars, to which were affiliated such bodies as the Knights of the Holy Spirit, the Occult Church of the Holy Grail, the Hermetic Brotherhood of Light, the Order of Enoch, the Rite of Memphis, and the Rite of Mizraim.

When Leo XIII died in 1903, and a conclave was called to elect his successor, Rampolla was known to be well in the running. His nearest rival was the Patriarch of Venice, Cardinal Sarto, a less impressive figure, as the world judges, but with an aura of goodness, or even natural saintliness about him, that Rampolla lacked.

At the first scrutiny, twenty-five votes were in his favour, while Sarto polled only five. As the voting proceeded the latter steadily increased his standing, but Rampolla continued to forge ahead. That seemed to have established the pattern of the voting, and, as though to accelerate its obvious result, the French Foreign Minister took the unusual step of requesting his countrymen among the Cardinals to back Rampolla.

Were hidden strings being pulled? Almost certainly they were. But if so the Sicilian's opponents, who may have been aware of his being a suspected Illuminatus, came forward with a last minute objection that dashed his claim. The Emperors of Austria, who were still recognised as legatees of the non-existent Holy Roman Empire, had been invested with the hereditary right to exercise a veto on candidates for the Papal throne whom they found unacceptable.

That veto was now expressed by the Cardinal of Cracow (a city that was then in Austria), in the name of the Emperor Franz Josef of Austria. Some said it was the veto of the Holy Ghost. Rampolla's hopes foundered, and the mind of the conclave swung round in favour of his nearest challenger, Sarto, who became Pope Pius X.

But it was not generally believed that the veto expressed by the 'very Catholic' Emperor of Austria was alone responsible for barring Rampolla's way, though he never, after the conclave, played any influential role in Rome.

After his death, Rampolla's papers passed into the keeping of Pius X. After reading them he put them aside with the comment: 'The unhappy man! Burn them.' The papers were put on the fire in the Pope's presence, but enough of them survived to furnish material for an article that appeared in *La Libre Parole*, in 1929 in Toulouse.

Some of the papers emanated from a secret society, the Order of the Temple of the Orient, and they provided proof that Rampolla had been working for the overthrow of Church and State. A notebook, discovered at the same time, throws a surprising sidelight on the possible Aleister Crowley connection; for several of the societies affiliated to the Temple of the Orient were those which have already been named, such as the Occult Church of the Holy Grail, and the Rite of Mizraim, in all of which Crowley exercised some great or small influence.

So it may have been that in the last days of world peace the secret societies came very near attaining, through Rampolla, their centuries-old goal — by claiming a Pope of their own.

9.

Growing chaos, and the replacement of traditional values by those of a new order, which were the tangible effects of the 1914 war, were seized upon as offering favourable opportunities to those who never ceased regarding the Church as their one great enemy. For early in 1936 a convention of secret societies was held in Paris; and although attendance was strictly limited to 'those in the know,' English and French observers managed to be present. Their accounts of the meeting appeared in the *Catholic Gazette* of February, 1936, and a few weeks later in *Le Réveil du Peuple,* a Paris weekly.

No one could fail to notice how closely the sentiments and topics that were there treated correspond to those put forward by Nubius and in the *Alta Vendita* more than a century before. What follows is a slightly shortened copy of the English version:

'As long as there remains any moral conception of the social order, and until all faith, patriotism, and dignity are uprooted, our reign over the world shall not come. We have already fulfilled part of our work, and yet we cannot claim that the whole of our work is done. We still have a long way to go before we can overthrow our main opponent, the Catholic Church.

'We must always bear in mind that the Catholic Church is the only institution which has stood, and which will, as long as it remains in existence, stand in our way. The Catholic Church, with its methodical work and her edifying moral teachings will always keep her children in such a state of mind as to make them too self-respecting to yield to our domination. That is why we have been striving to discover the best way of shaking the Catholic Church to her very foundations. We have spread the spirit of revolt and false liberalism among the nations so as to persuade them away from their faith and even to make them ashamed of professing the precepts of their religion, and obeying the commandments of their Church.

'We have brought many of them to boast of being atheists, and more than that, to glory in being descendants of the ape!

We have given them new theories, impossible of realisation, such as Communism, anarchism, and Socialism, which are now serving our purposes. They have accepted them with the greatest enthusiasm, without realising that those theories are ours, and that they constitute the most powerful instrument against themselves.

'We have blackened the Catholic Church with the most ignominious calumnies, we have stained her history, and disgraced even her noblest activities. We have imparted to her the wrongs of her enemies, and have brought these latter to stand more closely by our side. So much so that we are now witnessing, to our greatest satisfaction, rebellions against the Church in several countries. We have turned her clergy into objects of hatred and ridicule, we have subjected them to the hate of the crowd. We have caused the practice of the Catholic religion to be considered out of date and a mere waste of time. We have founded many secret associations which work for our purpose, under our orders and our directions.

'So far, we have considered our strategy in our attacks upon the Church from the outside. But this is not all. Let us explain how we have gone further in our work to hasten the ruin of the Catholic Church, and how we have penetrated into her most intimate circles, and have brought even some of her clergy to be pioneers of our cause:

'Apart from the influence of our philosophy, we have taken other steps to secure a breach in the Catholic Church. Let me explain how this has been done. We have induced some of our children to join the Catholic body with the explicit intention that they should work in a still more efficient way for the disintegration of the Catholic Church, by creating scandals within her.

'We are grateful to Protestants for their loyalty to our wishes, although most of them are, in the sincerity of their faith, unaware of their loyalty to us. We are grateful to them for the wonderful help they are giving us in our fight against the stronghold of Christian civilisation, and in our preparations for the advent of our supremacy over the whole world.

'So far we have succeeded in overthrowing most of the thrones of Europe. The rest will follow in the near future.

Russia has already worshipped our rule. France is under our thumb. England, in her dependence upon our finance, is under our heel; and in her Protestantism is our best hope for the destruction of the Catholic Church. Spain and Mexico are but toys in our hands. And many other countries, including the United States of America; have already fallen before our scheming.

'But the Catholic Church is still alive. We must destroy her without the least delay and without the slightest mercy.

Most of the Press of the world is under our control. Let us intensify our activities. Let us spread the spirit of revolution in the minds of the people.

'They must be made to despise patriotism and the love of their family, to consider their faith as a humbug, their obedience to the Church as a degrading servility, so that they may become deaf to the appeal of the Church and blind to her warnings against us. Let us, above all, make it impossible for Christians outside the Catholic Church to be re-united with her, or for non-Christians to join the Church; otherwise our domination over them will never be realised.'

Part Two

Our moral and political world is undermined with passages, cellars, and sewers.

Goethe.

The pontificate of Pius XII (1939-58) found the Church in a highly flourishing condition. It was exerting its legitimate effect upon the Western world. More and more people were acquiring a fuller realisation, or at least a glimmering, of the Catholic ideal. In England an average of ten thousand people yearly, and in the United States some seventy thousand in one year alone, were said to have 'gone over' to Rome; and these converts included not a few who could be classified as prominent in various walks of life.

Entire houses of Anglican religious, who had favoured High Church practices, sometimes followed suit. The record number of those training to be priests and nuns promised well for the Church's future. The tide of opposition , resulting from the Reformation was on the turn. The signs of Catholic revival were spreading throughout a most unexpected quarter-the English-speaking world.

Those things, strangely enough, coincided with the rise of Communism, and the widespread collapse of moral and social values that followed the 1939 war. During that war, which left Communism in the ascendant, the Vatican had been one of the few completely neutral centres in the world, which caused it to be adversely criticised by Communists who interpreted that attitude as latent partisanship for the other side; and that criticism was strengthened when the Pope passed sentence of excommunication on Catholics who joined, or in any way aided, the Communist Party.

This was an extension of the warning conveyed by the previous Pope, Pius XI, in his encyclical *Quadragesimo Anno*:

'No one can be at the same time a sincere Catholic and a Socialist properly so-called.'

Those words had doubtless been written with an eye on continental rather than English-speaking exponents of democracy. But they nonetheless implied condemnation, not only of revolutionary principles, but also of the milder forms of political expression that, when put to the test, encourage subversion.

There it was. The dividing line between Rome and her enemies had been firmly drawn. Both sides had issued their challenge and flourished their blazon. One was inspired by a Messianic though non-religious fervour that promised better things once the existing form of society had been dissolved; the other, secure in its reliance on a supernatural promise which meant that it would not, could not, compromise.

2.

The bishop in question was Angelo Giuseppe Roncalli. Born in 1881, and ordained in 1904, he soon attracted the notice of the Vatican, as a Doctor of Theology and a Professor of Ecclesiastical history. In 1921 he was assigned to the Congregation of Propaganda, and after being consecrated Bishop, in 1935, he entered the diplomatic service of the Church.

His first appointments were in the Balkan, a part of the world that was far from being favorably disposed towards any Catholic influence, as Roncalli discovered. As Apostolic Visitor, or *Chargé d'affaires* of the Holy See at Sofia, he became involved in diplomatic difficulties with the King, and these took on a more petty, but personal aspect when in 1935, he was transferred as Apostolic Delegate to Istanbul.

There the current fervor for modernisation, under Mustafa Kemal, was in full swing. Some of his laws came down heavily on religion, Islamic as well as Christian, and the wearing of any kind of clerical garb, in public was strictly forbidden. The use of ecclesiastical titles was also proscribed.

Roncalli was made to feel that he was in a kind of straitjacket, never really free but watched and spied on, and his moves reported. Any contacts he might have developed were few and far between, and his invariable habit, and the end of the day, was to go home quietly, a foreign and anonymous passer-by.

One evening he felt unusually tired, and without undressing or putting out the light, he flung himself on the bed. On the walls were reminders of his earlier life, the photographs of relatives, and of the village on the Lombardy plain where they had grown up together. He closed his eyes and murmured his usual prayers. In a kind of vision he saw the faces of people, those he had heedlessly passed on the street that day, float out of a mist before him. Among them was the face of an old man with white hair and an olive skin that gave him an almost oriental look.

What followed may have been a dream, or so it appeared to have been, when daylight came. But in the quiet room Roncalli distinctly heard the old man ask: 'Do you recognize me?' And without knowing what prompted him Roncalli answered: 'I do, Always.'

His visitor went on: 'I came because you called me. You are on the way, though you still have much to learn. But are you ready ?'

Roncalli never experienced the slightest doubt. It had all been prepared for him. He said: 'I wait for you Master.'

The old man smiled and asked three times, if Roncalli would recognized him again; and Roncalli answered three time, that he would.

Even the coming of morning did not make the experience seem unusual. It would, Roncalli knew, be repeated, in a way that would give it no ordinary meaning.

He knew that time had come when he found the same old man waiting outside his lodgings; and he also felt that a more familiar situation had developed, which caused Roncalli to ask if he would join him at table.

The old man shook his head. 'It is another table we must dine tonight." So saying he set off, with Roncalli following, into a quarter of quiet dark streets that the latter had never entered. A narrow opening led to a door at which Roncalli stopped, as if by instinct, while the old man told him to go up and wait for him.

Beyond the entrance was a short staircase, and then another. There was no light but in the almost total darkness there seemed to be voices from above, directing Roncalli's footsteps to go on. He was brought to a stop by a door, smaller than the others, which was slightly ajar, and Roncalli, pushing that open found himself in a wide room, pentagonal in shape, with bare walls and two large windows that were closed.

There was a big cedarwood table in the centre, shaped like the room. Against the walls were three chairs one holding a linen tunic, three sealed envelopes, and some coloured girdles. On the tables was a silver-hilted sword, the blade of which, in the partial light made by three red candles in a three-branched candelabra, appeared to be flaming. Three other candles in a second branched holder had not been lighted. There was a censer about which were tied coloured ribbons, and three artificial roses, made of flimsy material, and with their stalks crossing each other.

Near the sword and the censer was an open bible, and a quick glance was enough to show that it was open at the Gospel of St. John, telling the mission of John the Baptist, passages which had always held a peculiar fascination for Roncalli.

'A man appeared from God whose name was John...' The name John acquires a special significance in secret societies, who make a point of meeting on December 27th, the feast of the Evangelist, and on June 24th, feast day of the Baptist.

They frequently refer to the Holy Saints John.

Roncalli heard light footsteps behind him and turned from the table. It was someone he was to hear addressed, as Roncalli had called him, the master. He was wearing a long linen tunic that reached to the ground, and a chain of knots, from which hung various silver symbols, about his neck. He put a white-gloved hand on Roncalli's shoulder. 'Kneel down, on your right knee.'

While Roncalli was still kneeling the Master took one of the sealed envelopes from the chair. He opened it so that Roncalli was able to see that it contained a sheet of blue paper on which was written a set of rules. Taking and opening a second envelope the Master passed a similar sheet to Roncalli who, standing by them, saw it was inscribed with seven questions.

'Do you feel you can answer them?' asked the Master.

Roncalli said that he did, and returned the paper.

The Master used it to light one of the candles in the second holder. 'These lights are for the Masters of the Past[7] who are here among us,' he explained.

He then recited the mysteries of the Order in words that seemed to pass into and through Roncalli's mind without remaining there; yet he somehow felt, they had always been part of his consciousness. The master then bent over him.'

We are known to each other by the names we choose for ourselves. With that name each of us seals his liberty and his scheme of work, and so makes a new link in the chain. What will your name be?'

The answer was ready. There was no hesitation.

'Johannes,' said the disciple. Always ready to his mind, was his favourite Gospel.

The Master took up the sword, approached Roncalli, and placed the tip of the blade upon his head; and with its touch something that Roncalli could only liken to exquisite amazement, new and irrepressible, flowed into every part of his being. The Master sensed his wonder.

'What you feel at this moment, Johannes, many others have felt before you; myself, the Masters of the Past, and other brethren throughout the world. You think of it as light, but it has no name.'

They exchanged brotherly greetings, and the Master kissed the other seven times. Then he spoke in whispers, making Roncalli aware of the signs, gestures that have to be performed, and rites to be carried out daily, at precise moments, which correspond to certain stages in the passage of the sun.

'Exactly at those points, three times each day, our brethren all over the world are repeating the same phrases and making the

---

[7] The Masters are said to be perfect beings, the masters of humanity, who have passed through a series of initiations to a state of higher consciousness.

same gestures. Their strength is very great, and it stretches far. Day after day its effects are felt upon humanity.'

The Master took the remaining sealed envelope, opened it, and read the contents to Johannes. They concerned the formula of the oath, with a solemn undertaking not to reveal the Order's secrets, and to promise to work always for good, and most important of all, to respect the law of God and His ministers (a somewhat ambiguous stipulation in view of what their surroundings implied.)

Johannes appended his name to the paper, together with a sign and a number that the Master showed him. That confirmed his degree and entry into the Order; and once again a feeling of unearthly strength welled through his being.

The master took the paper, folded it seven times, and requested Johannes to place it on the point of the sword. Once again a sudden flame ran down the length of the blade. This was carried over to the candles that were still giving light 'for the Masters of the Past.'

The flames consumed it, and the master scattered the ashes. He then reminded Johannes of the solemnity of the oath he had taken, and how it would convey a sense of freedom, real freedom, that was known in general to the brethren. He then kissed Johannes, who was too overcome to respond by word or gesture, and could only weep.

A few weeks later Johannes (or Roncalli, as we must again continue to call him) was told that he was now sufficiently versed in the Cult to figure in its next conclusive phase — that of entering the Temple.

The master prepared him for what, he never disguised from Roncalli, would be an ordeal; and Roncalli's apprehension increased when he found that no one like himself, an initiate of only the first degree, was allowed to enter the Temple *unless a task of great importance was about to be entrusted to him.*

What could be ahead for Roncalli? Did the vision of a certain Chair, or throne, take shape in his mind as he made his way to the Temple?

There the brethren were assembled, another indication that Roncalli had been picked for some special mission. On the walls were the mysterious words, Azorth and Tetrammaton. The latter stands for the terrible, ineffable, and unpronounceable name of the creator of the universe, which was said to have been inscribed on the upper face of the cubicle, or foundation stone, in the Holy of Holies in the Temple at Jerusalem.

It figures in the pattern that is used for the evoking of evil spirits, or sometimes as a protection from them, a pattern that is known as the great magic circle is drawn between the two circles, which are composed of endless lines as symbolising eternity, various articles such as a crucifix, some herbs, and bowls of water, which is said to influence evil spirits, are placed.

Also in the temple was a cross, picked out in red and black, and the number 666, the number of the Beast in the Apocalypse. The Secret Societies, aware of the general ignorance regarding them, are now confident enough to show their hand. The American people are being made familiar with the mark of the beast on forms, brands of advertised goods, public notices: and is it mere coincidence that 666 is part of the code used in addressing letters to the British now serving (May 1982) in the South Atlantic (during the war with Argentina)? Those numbers, said to be all-powerful in the working of miracles and magic, are associated with the Solar God of Gnosticism.

The Gnostics, a Sect that flourished in the early Christian centuries, denied the divinity of Christ, disparaged revelation, and believed that all material things, including the body, were essentially evil. They held that salvation could only be achieved through knowledge (their name is derived from the Greek *gnosis* — knowledge). The Gospel stories they taught are allegories, the key to which is to be found in a proper understanding of Kneph, the sun god, who is represented as a serpent, and who is said to be the father of Osiris, and so the first emanation of the Supreme being, and the Christos of their Sect.

Roncalli, in his final and more elevated role for which the initiation prepared him, was to wear the image of the sun god surrounded by rays of glory, on his glove.

The colours red and black were held in reverence by the Gnostics and have been much in use by the diabolists. They are also the colours of Kali, the divine Mother of Hindu mythology; thus providing one of the several resemblances that occur between deviations from Christianity and pre-Christian cults. It may be noted that they figured on the banners of the International Anarchist Movement, whose prophet was Mikhail Bakunin (1814-1876), a pioneer of libertarianism as opposed to State socialism.

While Roncalli was noting the details of the room the brethren advanced from their places near the walls until they were drawing slowly and almost imperceptibly, closer, and closer to him. When they had formed a chain they pressed forward touching him with their bodies, as a sign that their strength, which had been tried and proven in earlier ceremonies, was being transmitted to him.

He suddenly realised that, without consciously framing them, he was being given words of power that streamed from him in a voice that he failed to recognise as his own. But he was able to see that everything he said was being written down by one who had been referred to as the Grand Chancellor of the Order. He wrote in French. On a sheet of blue paper that bore the heading 'The knight and the Rose.'[8]

Judging by that and other signs, it would appear that Roncalli was affiliated with the Rose-Croix, the Rosicrucians, a society founded by Christian Rosenkreutz, a German, who was born in 1378. But according to its own claims, 'The Order of the Rose and Cross has existed from time immemorial, and its mystic rites were practiced and its wisdom taught in Egypt. Eleusis, Samothrace, Persia, Chaldea, India, and in far, more distant

---

[8] A full account of Roncalli's initiation is given in *Les prophéties du pape John XXIII*, by Pierre Carpi, the pseudonym of an Italian who may have entered the same Order as Roncalli. It was translated into French, but is now very hard to find (Jean-Claude Lattes, Alta Books, 1975).

lands, and thus were handed down to posterity the Secret Wisdom of the Ancient Ages.'

That its origin remains a mystery was emphasised by (Prime Minister) Disraeli, who said of the Society, in 1841, 'Its hidden sources defy research.'

After travelling in Spain, Damascus and Arabia, where he was initiated into Arabian magic, Rosenkreutz returned to Germany and set up his fraternity of the *Invisibles*. In a building they designated as *Domus Sancti Spiritus* they followed such varied studies as the secrets of nature, alchemy, astrology, magnetism (or hypnotism as it is better known as) communication with the dead, and medicine.

Rosenkreutz is said to have died at the over-ripe age of 106, and when opened, his tomb which had been lost sight of for many years was found to contain signs and symbols of magic and occult manuscripts.

At first glance, Turkey may seem to be a country off the map: so far as the operations of a secret society are concerned.

But in 1911, Max Heindel, founder of the Rosicrucian Fellowship and the Rosicrucian Cosmo-Conception, wrote of that country in a manner that showed it was not escaping the observations of those who work with an eye on the religious, political, and social future. 'Turkey' he said, 'has taken a long stride towards liberty under the Young Turks of the Grand orient.'

During the last few decades we have learnt much, that was previously hidden, about the rites, passwords, and practices of the secret societies. But there are few indications of the way in which they choose, from their mainly inactive rank and file, those who are looked upon as capable of furthering their designs. One of their simple instructions runs: 'You must learn to govern men and dominate them, not by fear but by virtue, that is by observing the rules of the Order.' But an occult writing, which appeared in New York, is rather more explicit. 'Experiments are being made now, unknown oft to the subjects themselves ... people in many civilised countries are under supervision, and a method of stimulation and intensification is being applied by which they will bring to the knowledge of the Great Ones themselves a mass of information that may serve as guide to the future of the race. This was accompanied by a pointed remark that was also a pledge for one who had been judged to be suitable: 'You were long the object of our observation and our study.'[9]

---

[9] *Letters on Occult Meditation.* By Alice. A. Bailey. She was the High Priestess of an occult school and was associated with the Society of Illuminati minds.

3.

In the last days of December, 1944, Roncalli was preparing to leave Turkey for Paris, where he had been appointed Papal Nuncio to the Fourth French Republic. The war was still on, and the difference between Right and Left, in politics which had split France, was violently on the surface: and it became soon clear to observers whose judgement was not affected by ecclesiastical titles that Roncalli's innate sympathies were with the Left.

It was on his recommendation that Jacques Maritain was made French Ambassador to the Holy See. Maritain was generally regarded as a world thinker, certainly as one of the most prominent Catholic philosophers. The full impact of his 'integral humanism' had so far been tempered by his Aquinian perspective. But later it was overcome by such contemptuous promulgations as that the social kingship of Christ had been good enough for medieval minds (and Maritain's mentor, Thomas Aquinas, had been a medieval), but not for a people enlightened by such 'instruments' as the French and Bolshevist revolutions.

His status as a Catholic philosopher again causes doubt since, on his own testimony, he had been converted, not by any spiritual urge. Not by any theological or historical argument, by the writings of Leon Bloy (1846-1917).

In spite of its flowing musical style, Bloy's writing is hardly the sort of stuff to convert one to Christianity. He identified the Holy Ghost with Satan, and described himself as prophet of Lucifer, whom he pictured as seated on top of the world with his feet on the corners of the earth, controlling all human action, and exercising a fatherly rule over the swarm of hideous human offspring. Compared to this vision of an affable Lucifer, God is seen to be a relentless master whose work will end in final failure when Satan displaces Him as King.

According to his own confession, Bloy was converted to what he and his disciples called 'christianity' by the ravings of a poor prostitute who saw visions, and who after her affair with Bloy, died in a madhouse.

In 1947 Vincent Auriol was named President of the French Republic. He was an anti-Church plotter, one of those hardened anti-clericals who find a natural home on the continent; yet he and Roncalli became, not only cordial associates as their offices demanded, but close friends. This was not due to the Christian charity on one part and to diplomatic courtesy on the other, but to the ceremony that Roncalli had undergone in Istanbul, which established a bond of understanding between the two men.

This was given tangible expression when, in January 1953, Archbishop Roncalli was elevated to Cardinal and Aural insisted on exercising his traditional right, as the French head of State, to confer the red biretta on the newly created Prince of the Church. This occurred at a ceremony in the Elysee Palace, when Roncalli, seated on the chair (loaned by the museum) on which Charles X been crowned, received the plaudits of men who had sworn to bring him and all he stood for into dust, a design in which Roncalli was secretly pledged, though by more devious methods to assist them.

Three days later he was transferred, as Patriarch to Venice; and during the five years he was there he again showed, as in Paris, a certain sympathy for Left-wing ideologies that sometimes puzzled the Italian press.

It was during the pontificate of Pius XII that a number of priests then working in the Vatican became aware that all was not well beneath the surface. For a strange kind of influence not to their liking was making itself felt, and this they traced to a group who had come into prominence as experts, advisers, and specialists, who surrounded the Pope so closely that he was spoken of, half humorously, as being their prisoner.

But those priests who were more seriously concerned set up a chain of investigation, both here and in America, where their spokesman was Father Eustace Eilers, a member of the Passionist

Congregation of Birmingham, Alabama. This led to establishing the fact that the Illuminati were making themselves felt in Rome, by means of specially trained infiltrators who came from near the place in Germany where Adam Weishaupt had boasted of his plan to reduce the Vatican to a hollow shell. That the hand of the illuminati was certainly involved became clearer when Fr. Eilers, who announced that he was publishing those facts, was suddenly found dead, presumably one of those sudden heart attacks that, when dealing with secret societies, so often precede promised revelations.

Pius XII died on October 9, 1958, and on the 29th of that month. Angelo Roncalli, after Cardinals in conclave had voted eleven times, became the two hundred and sixty-second pope of the Catholic Church. He was seventy-seven, but with a build well able to sustain the sixty pounds of ecclesiastical vestments with which he was weighed down for his coronation on November 4th, 1958.

4.

Roncalli's 'election' was a signal for outbursts of welcome, often from the most unexpected quarters, to echo round the world. Non-Catholics, agnostics, and atheists agreed that the College of Cardinals had made an excellent choice, the best, in fact for many years. It lighted upon a man of wisdom, humility, and holiness, who would rid the church of superficial accretions and guide it back to the simplicity of Apostolic times; and last but not least among the advantages that promised well for the future, the new Pope was of peasant stock.

Seasoned Catholics could not account for the warmth and admiration that greeted him as journalists, correspondents, broadcasters, and television crews from almost every country in the world swarmed into Rome. For very little had hitherto been known to the outside world about Angelo Roncalli beyond the fact that he was born in 1881, had been Patriarch of Venice, and that he held diplomatic posts in Bulgaria, Turkey, and France. As for his humble background, there had been peasant popes before. The Church could absorb them as easily as it had her academic and aristocratic Pontiffs.

But the secular world, as evidenced by some of the most 'popular' publications in England, insisted that something momentous had happened in Rome, and that it was only the promise of still greater things to come; while informed Catholics, who for years had pleaded the Church's cause, continued to scratch their heads and wonder. Had some information gone forth, not to them who had always supported religion, but to those who have served up snippets of truth, or no truth at all, to titillate and mislead the public?

An Irish priest who was in Rome at the time said of the clamour for intimate details regarding Roncalli: 'Newspapers, and radio, television, and magazines, simply could not get enough information about the background and career, the family and the doings of the new Holy Father. Day after day, from the close of the conclave to the coronation, from his first radio message to the opening of the Consistory, the remarks and the activities of the new Pope were dealt out in flamboyant detail for all the world to see.'[10]

Speculation was added to interest when it became known that the new Pope wished to be known as John XXIII. Was it in memory of his father, who was named John, or out of respect for John the Baptist? Or was it to emphasise his readiness to outface or even to shock the traditional outlook? John had been a favourite name for many Popes. But why retain the numbering?

For there had been an earlier John XXIII, an anti-pope, who was deposed in 1415. He has a tomb in the baptistry at Florence, and his portrait appeared in the *Annuario Pontifico*, the Church's yearbook, until recent years. It has since been removed. We know nothing to his credit, for his only recorded achievement, if the word of such a precious reprobate as himself can be believed, was to have seduced more than two hundred women including his sister-in-law.

Meantime there was a general feeling abroad that the Church was approaching a break with the traditional past. It had always evinced a proud refusal to be influenced by its environment. It had been protected, as by some invisible armour, from the fashion of the time. But now it was showing a readiness to undergo a self-imposed reformation as dramatic as that, which had been forced upon it in the sixteenth century. To some it was anticipated as a bringing up to date of Christian doctrine, a desirable and inevitable process of re-conversion, in which a deeper and ever expanding catholicity would replace the older and static Catholicism of the past.

---

[10] *John XXIII, the Pope from the Fields,* by Father Francis X. Murphy. (Hebert Jenkins, 1959.)

Such a change was guardedly foreshadowed in an early statement by John XXIII when he said: 'Through east and west there stirs a wind, as it was born of the spirit arousing the attention and hope in those who are adorned with the name of Christians.'

The words of 'Good Pope John' (how quickly he acquired that complimentary assessment) were not merely prophetic.

For they spoke of changes in the once monumental Church that would be initiated by himself.

5.

American collectors of ecclesiastical mementoes would have noticed, soon after Pope John's election, that certain objects were being offered for sale in some of their papers. They were described as copies of the personal cross chosen and sanctioned by John XXIII.

These crosses had nothing to do with the pectoral cross that is worn, suspended from the neck, by every Pontiff and Bishop as a sign of episcopal authority. They are made of gold, ornamented with precious stones, and each one contains a holy relic. Before wearing it the prelate says a prescribed prayer in memory of the Passion, and begs for grace to overcome the wiles of the Evil One throughout the day.

But the cross that was put before the American public, under Roncalli's patronage, had very different associations. For its centre, instead of holding a representation of the crucified Figure, contained the all-seeing Eye of the Illuminati, enclosed in a triangle or pyramid; and these crosses, advertised in *The Pilot* and *The Tablet*, the diocesan papers of Brooklyn and of Boston, were, in keeping with the lack of dignity and reverence that was becoming proverbial, on sale at two hundred and fifty dollars each.

Those who understood the meaning of the mystic symbols, and how profoundly they affect us, again had their attention drawn to the sun-face that was depicted on John's glove. It was reminiscent of the design used by pagan sun worshippers; while his gesture of extending a hand, with fingers spread over a congregation, could also be recognised as an invocation to the white moon, part of an esoteric code that has always claimed followers.

To those who think that such suggestions verge on the ridiculous, it need only be pointed out that thousands of sedate, bowler hatted businessmen have, in the course of furthering their careers, performed rituals and adopted symbols that make the above seem very tame indeed.

To people in general, however, the pyramid, without resigning one jot of its original significance, now passes as a thoroughly respectable and harmless sign. It is merely a decoration. But it is one that goes into general circulation whenever an American one dollar note changes hands.

For on the reverse side of the note is the secret Eye, enclosed in a pyramid, and the date 1776. There are also the words *Annuit Coeptis, Novus Ordo Seclorum*.

The date 1776 may indicate no more to the unsuspecting than that it was the year of the Declaration of American Independence, drawn up by Thomas Jefferson.

True enough. But what of the symbols, which also figure on the reverse side of the Great Seal of the United States-why choose them? And 1776 was also the year in which Adam Weishaupt founded his brotherhood. And Thomas Jefferson, like his fellow politician Benjamin Franklin, was an ardent Illuminist.

The words quoted above may be translated as meaning: 'He (God) has approved of our undertaking, which has been crowned with success. A new order of the ages is born.'

It has been demonstrated, time and again, that the future of the world is in the hands not of mere politicians, but of those who have the power, occult allied to international financial power, to manipulate events according to their plans; and we of the present time have witnessed the coming of their new order in several departments of life, including the religious, political, and social. Before the current propaganda that emphasises the role of women became popular, the occult authority Oswald Wirth spoke of woman 'not being afraid' to adopt masculine rites and customs, and of how, when she has obtained her full power, men will comply with her directions. That process is being actively carried out before us.

The term 'new' is being propagated as though it necessarily implies a marked improvement in whatever has existed before. It attained political prominence in 1933, the year in which Roosevelt's New Deal was instituted; and it was in that same year that the Illuminati insignia, with the words referring to the 'new order of the ages,' appeared on the reverse side of the American dollar bill. Their enactment is now taking shape in the formation of a new One World Order in which, it is anticipated, different nations, races, cultures, and traditions will be absorbed to the point of eventually disappearing.

Part Three

I am certain that when in the Council I pronounced the ritual words 'Exeunt Omnes' (everyone out) one who did not obey was the Devil. He is always there where confusion triumphs, to stir it up and take advantage of it.

Cardinal Pericle Felici,
Secretary-General of the Council.

With a truly amazing foresight that was born of confidence, the secret societies had long since made up their minds how they would bring about changes in the claims and character of the Catholic Church, and ultimately its downfall. More than a century ago they recognised that the policy of infiltration, by which their own men were entering the highest places in the ecclesiastical structure had met with success; and now they could outline the nature of the next stage to be accomplished.

Speaking as one of the arch-plotters who was 'in the know,' Giuseppe Mazzini (1805-72) said: 'In our time humanity will forsake the Pope and have recourse to a General Council of the Church.' Mazzini was not immune to the drama of the anticipated situation, and went on to speak of the 'Papal Caesar' being mourned as a victim for the sacrifice, and of an executed termination.

A similar note was struck by Pierre Virion who wrote in *Mystère d'Iniquité:* 'There is a sacrifice in the offing which represents a solemn act of expiation.... The Papacy will fall. It will fall under the hallowed knife which will be prepared by the Fathers of the last Council.'

A former canon-lawyer, Roca, who had been unfrocked for heresy, was more explicit. 'You must have a new dogma, a new religion, a new ministry, and new rituals that very closely resemble those of the surrendered Church.' And Roca was not merely expressing a hope, but describing a process. 'The divine cult directed by the liturgy, ceremonial, ritual and regulations of the Roman Catholic Church will shortly undergo transformation at an ecumenical Council.'

One evening early in 1959, when he had been Pope for scarcely three months, John XXIII was walking in the Vatican Gardens.

His slow and weighty perambulations under the oaks and horse chestnuts, where Pius IX had ridden on his white mule, were suddenly broken in upon by what he was to call an impulse of Divine Providence, a resolution that reached him from beyond, and whose impact he recognised.

A Council-he almost breathed the words-he was to call a General Ecumenical Council of the Church.

Later he said that the idea had not been inspired by any revelation of the Holy Spirit but through a conversation he had with Cardinal Tardini, then Secretary of State, towards the end of the previous year. Their talk had turned on what could be done to present the world with an example of universal peace. But there was still some confusion as to the origin of the thought, for Pope John subsequently said that he framed it himself, in order to let a little fresh air into the Church.

Councils in the past had been called to resolve some crisis in the Church, some burning question that threatened a split or to confuse opinion. But no such question, related to doctrine or discipline, was pressing for an answer in the early part of 1959. The Church was exacting its traditional dues of loyalty, neglect, or antagonism. There appeared to be no need to summon a Council. Why cast a stone into peaceful waters that, sooner or later, were bound to be disturbed by obvious necessity? But Pope John, on January 25th, announced his intention to the College of

Cardinals; and the response it evoked in the secular world soon made it clear that this was to be no ordinary Council.

The same measure of unexampled publicity that marked the election of John XXIII, welcomed the plan. It was made to appear a matter of moment not only to the non-Catholic world, but to elements that had always strongly opposed Papal claims, dogma, and practice. But few wondered at this sudden show of interest on the part of agnostics; still fewer would have suspected a hidden motive. And if a small voice expressing doubt managed to be heard it was soon silenced as preparations for the first session of the Council went ahead.

They occupied two years, and consisted of the drawing up of drafts, or schemas, on decrees and constitutions that might be deemed worthy of change. Each member of the Council, which would consist of Bishops drawn from every part of the Catholic world, and presided over by the Pope or his legate, could vote for the acceptance, or rejection, of the matter discussed; and each was invited to send in a list of debatable subjects.

Some days before the Council opened, it appeared that the authorities responsible for it had been assured that this mainly Catholic affair would be given more than its usual share of normal publicity. A greatly enlarged Press office was set up facing St. Peter's. Cardinal Cicognani officiated at its opening and gave it his blessing; and the gentlemen of the Press poured in.

They included a surprising number of atheistic Communists who arrived, like hunters, expecting to be 'in' at a kill. The *Soviet Literary Gazette*, which had never before been represented at any religious gathering, took the surprising step of sending a special correspondent in the person of a certain M. Mchedlov, who smoothed his way into Rome by expressing the most heart-felt admiration for the Pope. Two of Mchedlov's fellow-countrymen were there, in the shape of a reporter from the Soviet news-agency *Tass*, and another from the Moscow periodical which was frankly named *Communist*. Another prominent member of the Bolshevik clan was M. Adjubei, who besides being editor of

Izvestia was son-in-law to the Soviet Prime Minister, Khrushchev.

He was given a warm welcome by Good Pope John, who invited him to a special audience at the Vatican. News of this promising reception was sent to Khrushchev, who straightway noted his intention of sending greetings to the Pope on November 25th, 1963, his next birthday. An unknown number of Italians, when they recovered from their surprise at seeing the Head of the Church on friendly terms with its enemies, decided to cast their votes in favour of Communism at the next opportunity.

This resolve was strengthened when a special number of *Propaganda,* the organ of the Italian Communist Party, helped to swell the chorus of praise for the coming Council. Such an event, it said, would be comparable to the opening of the States General, the curtain raiser to the French Revolution, in 1789. With the same theme in mind, the paper likened the Bastille (which fell in that same year) to the Vatican, which was about to be shaken to its very foundations.

More Left-wing approval came from Jacques Mitterrand, Master of the French Grand Orient, who knew that he could safely praise, in advance, Pope John and the effects of the Council in general.

Among the Russian Orthodox observers was the young Bishop Nikodim who, in spite of maintaining a strict religious standing, was apparently free to come and go through the Iron Curtain.

Two other Bishops from his part of the world, one Czech and one Hungarian, joined him and Cardinal Tisserant at a secret meeting that was held at a place near Metz, shortly before the Council's first session. Nikodim, a somewhat shady figure, needs to be remembered since he appears later in these pages.

We' know now that the Russians dictated their own terms for 'sitting in' at the Council. They intended to use it as a means for broadening their influence in the Western world, where Communism had been condemned thirty-five times by Pius XI, and no less than 123 times by his successor Pius XII. Popes John and Paul VI were to follow suit, but each, as we shall see, with tongue in cheek. It was now Russian policy to see that the Bulls of Excommunication issued against Catholics who joined the Communist Party were silenced, and that no further attack on Marxism would be made at the Council. On both points the Kremlin was obeyed.

The Council, made up of 2,350 Bishops, sixty from Russian controlled countries, opened on October the 11th, 1962.

They formed an impressive procession, with the greatest array of mitres seen in our time as their wearers passed through the bronze door of St. Peter's; guardians of the Faith, protectors of tradition, on the march; assertive men, confident of their stand, and therefore capable of inspiring confidence, and opposition.... Or so they were in appearance. Few who saw them could have guessed that many of those grave and reverend Fathers were, according to the rules of the Church whose vestments they wore, and at whose bidding they had come together, excommunicate and anathema. The mere suggestion would have been laughed at.

2.

With the preliminaries over, the Council members were free to question, discuss, and compare notes as they met at the various coffee bars that had been opened; and already a more sober and reflective mood, distinct from that with which many had greeted the calling of the Council, was passing over the assembly. In some cases it was near disillusionment. It was not only a matter of language, though many different ones were, of course, being spoken. But some of those present seemed to have had little grounding, not only in Latin, but in the essentials of their Faith. Their background was not that of the orthodox, traditional Catholic; and those who were part of that background, and who were familiar with the writings of Heidegger and Jean-Paul Sartre could detect, in the statements and even casual remarks made by all too many prelates, the equivocations and lack of authority habitual to men who are the products of modern thought.

More than that, some let it be known that they did not believe in Transubstantiation, and therefore not in the Mass. But they held firmly by Nietzsche's pride in life, and the deification of human reason, while rejecting the idea of an Absolute, and the concept of creation.

One Bishop from Latin America expressed his bewilderment mildly by saying that many of his fellow prelates appear to have lost their faith.' Another was frankly horrified to discover that some to whom he had spoken, and who had but temporarily put aside their mitres, scorned any mention of the Trinity and the Virgin Birth. Their background owed nothing to the Thomist philosophy, and one veteran of the Curia, inured to the firmness of the Roman pavement, made short work of the Council Fathers by summing them up as 'two thousand good-for-nothings.' There were some among the bitterly disillusioned who said they would merely put in a token appearance for a week or two, and then go home.

Representatives from the Middle East recalled a warning that had been uttered by Salah Bitah, the Premier of Syria, when first he heard that the Council was being called. He had reason to believe that the Council was nothing but an 'international plot.' Others supported that definition by producing a book, which had been handed to them on landing at the airport, in which it was said that the Council was part of a plan to destroy the Church's doctrine and practice, then, ultimately, the Institution itself.

The general tone of the Council was soon set, with the 'good-for nothings,' or progressives, as they came to be called, clamouring for modernisation and a revision of values within the Church, and a far less active, and much less vocal opposition, offered by their traditionalist, or orthodox, opponents. The difference between the two sides was stressed at the opening of the first session, when the progressives addressed their own particular message to the world, to ensure that the Council 'started off on the right foot.'

Pope John followed that up by declaring that the ashes of St. Peter were thrilling in 'mystic exaltation,' because of the Council. But not all his listeners, and certainly not the conservatives among them, were smiling. Perhaps they already sensed defeat as they looked at some of the Cardinals, Suenens, Lienart, Alfrink, and such prominent theologians as the Dominican Yves Congar, who contributed to French Left-wing papers; the ultra-liberal Schillebeeckx, also Dominican, and Professor of Dogmatic Theology at the University of Nijmegen; and Marie-Dominique Chenu whose writings, as when he said that 'Marx's great analysis enriches both today and tomorrow with his current of thought,' had brought a frown to the forehead of Pius XII; all hot in pursuit of progress, and none too careful in the choice of weapons they used to attain it.

Another of those influential figures was Montini, Archbishop of Milan, who drew up and supervised the documents relating to the early stages of the Council. His reputation was increasing daily. He was obviously a man of the future.

The silence of the passive minority, a silence that admitted defeat at the outset, was communicated to Pope John, who put it down to the awe and solemnity inspired by the occasion.

3.

These pages will not attempt to summarise the day-to-day work of the Council. They will instead seek to point out how faithfully the Council fulfilled the purposes of those progressives, liberals, infiltrators (call them what you will), who had brought it into being; and the less efficient, less determined attitude of their opponents.

The former group, made up largely of German-speaking Bishops, had from the first been active behind the scenes. They had audiences with the Pope and discussed changes in the liturgy and other subjects they had in mind. They altered the rules of procedure to suit their policy, and ensured that the various commissions were made up of those who shared their outlook. They distorted, or suppressed, any issue that did not suit their purpose. They blocked the appointment of opponents to any position where their voices might be heard, discarded resolutions that did not please them, and took over the documents on which deliberations were based.

They were supported by the Press, which was, of course, controlled by the same power as that which added fuel to the flames of infiltration. Apart from that, the German Bishops financed their own news agency. And so, in reports that reached the public, the Left-wing Bishops were depicted as honest, brilliant, and men of towering intellect, whereas those in the opposite camp were stupid, feeble, stubborn, and out-of-date. The Left, moreover, had the might of the Vatican behind it, and a weekly news-letter, written by Montini, which set the tone of the way in which debatable issues would be resolved by the Council. His remarks on liturgical reform were popularised by the Press and welcomed by those who wished to see the Mass reduced to the level of a meal between friends.

On looking back at this time of day, one is forced to wonder at the negligence, or weakness, with which their traditional or orthodox opponents confronted moves that, to men of their profession, threatened the very purpose of their existence. They were not ignorant of what had been planned, and of what was then going on. They knew that a forceful Fifth Column, many of them mitred members of the hierarchy, were working for the downfall of the Western Church. But they did nothing beyond observing protocol, and overcoming whatever resentment they felt by an inbred obedience. It was almost as though (allowing that morality was on their side) they wished to exemplify the saying: 'Good men are feeble and tired; it is the blackguards who are determined.'

A factor that helped to decide the situation was that of age. Most of the Council Fathers belonging to the old traditional school had passed their prime; and they now, like Cardinal Ottaviani, whose name had once been weighty in the Curia, counted for little more than an almost despised rearguard.

An unconscious recognition of this was made by another of their number, the aged Bishop of Dakar, who shook his head over the dictatorial method by which the modernists, even in the preliminary stages of the Council, swept all before them. 'It was,' he said, 'organised by a master mind:'

For their part, the modernists were frankly contemptuous of everything mooted by the orthodox elements in the Council. When one of their propositions came up for tentative discussion, one updated' Council Father declared that those who put it forward 'deserved to be shot to the moon.' But even so the Russian observers, despite early signs that the Council was prepared to toe the Communist line, were not wholly satisfied, though John XXIII was praised for maintaining his independence, and for not becoming a cats-paw of the Right.

But the Tass correspondent regretted the presence of too many 'obvious reactionaries' in the assembly, a sentiment that was echoed by M. Mchedlov who added: 'So far the die-hard conservatives have failed to carry the day. They have not succeeded in turning the Church into a tool of their reactionary propaganda.'

4.

Between the ending of the first session of the Council on the 1st of December 1962, and the opening of the second session on September the 29th of the following year, Pope John, after a protracted illness, breathed his last on the evening of Monday, June the 3rd, 1963; and every form of publicity, which over the past weeks had delivered a breath-by-breath account of the deathbed in Rome, again swung into action to extol a man who had faithfully served the purpose for which he had been given the occupancy of Peter's Chair, and set in motion a series of events that were directed to fulfil, at the expense of the Church, a large part of the aims determined by secret societies over the centuries.

A prominent member of the conspiracy that had fostered John XXIII, the ex-doctor of Canon Law, Roca, commented drily: 'The old Pope, having broken the silence and started the tradition of the great religious controversy, goes to his grave;' while a revealing tribute, which should open the eyes of anyone who still finds offence in the mention of a plot, was written by Charles Riandey, a sovereign Grand Master of secret societies, in his preface to a book by Yves Marsaudon,[11] State Minister of the Supreme Council of French secret societies: 'To the memory of Angelo Roncalli, priest, Archbishop of Messamaris, Apostolic Nuncio in Paris, Cardinal of the Roman Church, Patriarch of Venice, Pope under the name of *John XXIII*, who has deigned to give us his benediction, his understanding, and his protection' *(my emphasis)*.

---

[11] Ecumenism as seen by a French freemason. (Paris, 1969).

A second preface to the book was addressed to 'his august continuer, His Holiness Pope Paul VI'.

Never before had the passing of a Pope, in the person of John XXIII, been so extensively covered. Tough reporters wept at the news. The fingers of sensation-hardened columnists fumbled over their typewriter keys. Only a very few, who knew what had happened in the dark room in Istanbul, stood with heads unbowed and with minds uncluttered by propaganda, reflecting that Angelo Roncalli had indeed, as the pious used to say, 'gone to his reward.'

The question of his successor was never seriously in doubt. The calling of a conclave was little more than a formality. The same voices that had eulogised the Rosicrucian John XXIII now clamoured for Montini, Montini of Milan. Anglicans, who had no time for a Pope of any or of no policy whatever, agreed that Montini was the man.

He had, in fact, been prepared and coached for the office by Pope John, who created Montini his first Cardinal, whereas Pius XII had always withheld the red hat from one whom he knew to be pro-Communist. Montini had been the only non-resident Cardinal whom John invited to live in the Vatican, where they exchanged intimate and unofficial talks over the results they both anticipated from the Council; and Pope John packed the College of Cardinals to ensure that Montini, as his successor, would continue to promulgate the heretical decrees that they both favoured.

The most spirited protests against the election were made by Joaquin Saenz Arriaga, Doctor of Philosophy and of Canon Law, who scented danger in the fact that a large part of Montini's support came from secular commentators who were not concerned with the welfare, but with the downfall of the Church. Some of his credentials and qualifications were said to have been exaggerated, or false.

However, the decision of a conclave, established by usage, could not be questioned; and Montini, who took the name of Paul VI, was elected on June the 23rd, 1963.

5.

Giovanni Battista Montini was one of those socialists who, although born in far from humble circumstances themselves, are quick to resent the slightest sign of privilege in others. He was born on September 26th, 1897, in Northern Italy, into a highly professional family (of likely Hebrew origin) that, more than a century before, had been accepted into the annals of Roman nobility.

His father, Giorgi Montini, a prominent Christian Democrat, in all probability belonged to a secret society, which would partly account for his son's later commitment. Showing early signs of wishing to enter the Church, the young Giovanni was of such a delicate constitution that he was allowed to study at home instead of at a seminary, which left him free to develop social and political trends that were not those of a normally trained and disciplined servant of the Church.

By the time he entered upon his first regular appointment as a university chaplain in Rome he was an established man of the Left. But that did not prevent his steady and undoubted ability to rise in a conservative atmosphere, and he became acting Vatican Secretary of State under Pius XII.

Montini had long been an admirer of the works of the philosopher Jacques Maritain, whose system of 'Integral Humanism,' with its rejection of authoritarian and dogmatic belief in favour of a world-wide fraternity which would include non-believers, had earned the approval of John XXIII.

Man, according to Maritain, was essentially good, an outlook that made him less responsive to the vital distinction that exists between man-made secular forms of existence and the demands made by belief in the divine nature of Christ and of the Church.

Both Maritain and Montini rejected the traditionalist view of the Church as the one means of attaining true world unity. It might have appeared so in the past, but now a new world, more sensitive to and capable of solving social and economic problems, had come into existence. And Montini, whom Maritain regarded as his most influential disciple, spoke for all of their persuasion when he said: 'Do not be concerned with church bells. What is necessary is that priests are able to hear the factory sirens, to understand the temples of technology where the modern world lives and thrives.' There is a document the contents of which, so far as I know, have seldom if ever been made available to the public. It is dated September the 22nd, 1944, after having been reported on the previous August 28th, and based on information given on July 13th of the same year. It is now among the records of the Office of Strategic Services, which later became the Central Intelligence Office, the C.I.A.[12]

It is headed: 'Togliatti and the Vatican make first direct contact,' and deals with the plans for social and economic revolutions that were being worked out between the Church and one of its most consistent enemies, the Communist Party.

Here it is quoted: On July 10th, at the house of a Christian Democrat Minister, the acting Vatican Secretary of State, Monsignor Giovanni Montini, conferred with Togliatti, Communist Minister without Portfolio, in the Bonomi Government. Their conversation reviewed the grounds out of which have grown the understanding between the Christian Democratic and the Communist Parties.

Since his arrival in Italy, Togliatti had private meetings with politicians of the Christian Democratic Party. These contacts constituted the political background of Togliatti's speech at the Teatro Brancaccio on Sunday, July 9th, and account for the warm reception the speech received from the Catholic Press.

---

[12] It was brought to my notice by Mr. Michael Gwynn of the Britons Library.

'Through leaders of the Christian Democratic Party, Togliatti was able to convey to the Vatican his impression of Stalin's opinion on religious freedom, as now accepted by Communism, and of the democratic character of the agreement between Russia and the Allied nations. On the other hand, the Holy See reached Togliatti through the same means, and expressed its opinion regarding the future agreement with Soviet Russia on the matter of Communism in Italy, as well as in other nations.

'The discussion between Monsignor Montini and Togliatti was the first direct contact between a high prelate of the Vatican and a leader of Communism. After having examined the situation, they acknowledged the practical possibility of a contingent alliance between Catholics and Communists in Italy, which should give the three parties (Christian Democrat, Socialist, and Communist) an absolute majority, thereby enabling them to dominate any political situation.

A tentative plan was drafted to form the basis on which an agreement between the Christian Democrat Party and the Communist and Socialist Parties could be made. They also drafted a plan of the fundamental lines along which a practical understanding between the Holy See and Russia, in their new relations, could be created.'

To sum up, Montini informed Togliatti that the Church's antiCommunist stand should not be considered as something lasting, and that many in the Curia wished to enter into talks with the Kremlin.

These meetings with the enemy displeased Pius XII, who came to eye his Secretary of State with a growing disfavour; and Montini, for his part, searched for a chink in the Pope's armour. He found one in the fact that Pius had secured lucrative posts for some of his nephews; and Montini played -upon this evidence of Papal nepotism for all it was worth, much to the delight of his socialistic, anti-clerical comrades.

Pius responded by dismissing Montini from his confidential post, and sending him north as Archbishop of Milan. That office had previously been filled, as of right, by a Cardinal; but there was no red hat, until 1958, for Montini.

There he was free to make full play with his political sympathies, which came to shift more obviously to the Left. Some of his writings, which appeared in the diocesan paper, *L'Italia*, made some of his priests wary of their superior, and before long more than forty of them withdrew their subscriptions to the paper. But their disapproval meant little or nothing to Montini who, with Maritain in the background, had come upon a more active supporter of his ultra-liberal opinions.

This was Saul David Alinsky, a typical representative of the agitator type who affect to nurse a deep-seated grievance against the capitalistic circles in which they are always careful to move, and on whose bounty they flourish.

Montini was so impressed by Alinsky's brand of revolutionary teaching-he was known as the Apostle of Permanent Revolution that the two spent a fortnight together, discussing how best to bring the demands of the Church, and those of the Communist unions, into line with each other. It must be remarked that Alinsky was as singularly fortunate in his personal relations as he was in his financial backers. For at the end of their talks Montini declared that he was pleased to call himself one of Alinsky's best friends; while Jacques Maritain, in a mood that revealed the softening up process that his philosophic outlook must have undergone, said that Alinsky was one of the 'few really great men of the century.'

One of Alinsky's rich backers-and this advocate of the class warfare had several, including such odd combinations as the Rockefeller foundation and the Presbyterian Church-was the millionaire Marshall Field. This latter contact had served as a further aid to strengthen Alinsky's image in Montini's eyes, since Marshall Field, who had published a Communist newspaper, sponsored various subversive movements, and had waltzed his way through two divorce courts and three matrimonial cases, had remained a faithful son of the Church-his bank balance saw to that-and was an intimate friend of Bishop Shiel of Chicago.

At the same time Montini established a relationship, at first merely business, that was to have far reaching effects throughout much of Italy, including the Vatican, in the not too distant future. In the course of dealing with the complicated financial affairs of the Church he encountered a shady character, Michele Sindona, who was running a tax consultant's office (that at least was part of his many-sided operations) in Milan.

Sindona was a Sicilian, born in 1917, a product of the heterogeneous Jesuit training who was studying law when British and American troops invaded the island during the second world war. Another scourge that the war enabled to renew itself in Sicily was the Mafia.

Driven underground by Mussolini, it had since emerged, with its proverbially strong American support and an obliging hand provided by President Roosevelt who, like practically every one of the American presidents since the time of Washington (himself an Illuminatus) was an active supporter of secret society ramifications. One of Roosevelt's several titles was Knight of Pythias, which proclaimed membership of a society based on the mythical pair of pagans, Damon and Pythias; while he was also a wearer of the red fez as one of the Ancient Arabic Order of Nobles of the Mystic Shrine.

Sindona thrived on the ugly conditions engendered by the Mafia and the war. He obtained a truck, and made a good living by peddling oddments and minor necessities to the troops. It is doubtful whether, as some say, he took part in lodging information against the Germans, and helping to sabotage their positions. But he soon became one with the gangster element surrounding the American army commanders, who made their rounds in a luxury car presented to them, in return for services rendered, by the Mafia.

Protected and patronised by the Allies, Sindona was soon at the head of a flourishing black market racket; and when the war ended, following the trail of those who had sharpened his appetite for money, he turned his back upon the indigent south and went to Milan, where he met an apt collaborator in the Archbishop.

Montini's coming to power was marked by the arrival in Rome of people who fairly dismayed the more conventional lookers-on at Vatican ceremonial; and since the Roman nature is too sharp for simple hypocrisy, they more than sniffed disapproval of the pimpish publicity men, pseudo-artists of every type, out-of conscience clerics, and miscellaneous hangers-on who flocked south and pitched their metaphorical tents under the shadow of St. Peter's cupola.

Rome, Montini's critics declared, was again being invaded by barbarians from the north.

Others said it was the Mafia. They were not far wrong. For among the new arrivals was Michele Sindona, no longer trundling a barrow, but lolling in a shiny chauffeur-driven car and doubtless appraising the Papal and imperial monuments he passed with the eye of a businessman.

6.

Pope John, speaking for the Council he had called and referring to its purpose, had said: 'Our greatest concern is that the sacred deposit of Catholic doctrine should be guarded.' The Church must never depart 'from the sacred patrimony of truth received from the Fathers.'

There was nothing strange or revolutionary in that. So much had been taken for granted from generation to generation. But as the Council got underway the Pope changed his tune, and spoke of the Church not being concerned with the study of old museums or symbols of thought from the past. 'We live to advance. We must evermore move forward. The Christian life is not a collection of ancient customs'; and Pope Paul, not many hours after being elected, announced his intention of consolidating and implementing his predecessor's Council, and in a way, as we shall see, that endorsed the second of Pope John's statements.

So far as the general reader is concerned, the most outstanding result achieved by the Council was the changed relationship between atheistic Communism and the Church; and the fact that such a surprising turnabout was effected shows that Mazzini and his fellow conspirators had not miscalculated when, so many years before, they had pinned their hopes of fatally undermining the Church on a General Council. It also illustrates the methods employed by those who, however exalted their ecclesiastical titles, were first and foremost the endorsers of the secret revolutionary creed.

The schema on Communism was welcomed by the Polish Cardinal Wyszynsky, who had had personal experience of life behind the Iron Curtain. Six hundred Council Fathers supported him, and 460 signed a petition requesting that condemnation of the atheistic materialism, that was enslaving part of the world, should be renewed.

Yet when the Commission's report on the Church in the modern world was made known, the substance of the petition was not referred to; and when those responsible for it pressed for an explanation, they were told that only two votes had been cast against Communism.

But what, asked some of the astonished and disappointed signatories, had happened to the much greater number who had favoured the petition? They were informed that the matter had not been brought to the notice of all the Council Fathers, since some 500 of them had gone to Florence, where celebrations in honour of Dante were being held.

Still not satisfied, those who had been so obviously outmanoeuvred pressed the Jesuit Robert Tucci, a prominent member of the appropriate Commission, for an explanation. Their suspicions were groundless, he told them. There had been no bargaining, no back-stairs intrigue. It could only mean that the petition had 'run into a red light on the way,' and so had come to a standstill.

Another explanation was that the intervention had not arrived within the prescribed time limit, and so had escaped notice.

The argument went on, with two of the Council Fathers declaring that they had personally delivered the signed intervention to the General Secretariat on time; and when that was proved to be correct, there was a climb-down on the part of those who had so far blocked the condemnation of Communism.

Archbishop Garonne of Toulouse was called in to square matters, and he admitted the timely arrival of the petition, together with negligence on the part of those who should have transmitted the matter to members of the Commission. Their failure to do so meant that the petition had not been examined. But there was more inconsistency even on the part of those who admitted error.

The Archbishop said that 332 interventions had been handed in. Another quoted the number of 334, but that was also contradicted when it was announced that the total to arrive on time had been 297.

There was one more attempt on the part of those who wished the Church's original condemnation of Communism to be reaffirmed. It figured as a request to check the names of the 450 prelates who had signed the petition. But that was turned down. The petition had been added to the collected documents relating to the case, and they were simply not available. So, as in all such matters, the traditionalists lost heart. Their cause flickered out and the modernists, confident as ever, remained in possession of the field.

Their victory, and that of the secret societies who manipulated the Council, had been pre-figured by Cardinal Frings, one of the German-speaking consortium, when he said that any attack on Communism would be stupid and absurd, sentiments that were echoed by the internationally controlled Press. And at the same time, as though to cast light on the far reaching surrender made by the Church to its enemy (which many people, a few years back, would have judged unthinkable), Josef Cardinal Beran, the exiled Archbishop of Prague who was then living in Rome, received a cutting from a Czecho-Slovakian paper.

In it, one of their political creed boasted that Communists had been able to infiltrate all the Commissions that were steering the course of the Council; a claim that was well borne out when tactics similar to those described were employed, with equal success, at every stage of the sittings.

A typical instance was during the debate on the Religious Orders. Right-wing speakers, who had previously made known their intention to speak, were not allowed the use of the microphone. But it was made available to their opponents of the Left whose names had only been handed in that morning. Those indignant that having been silenced pressed for an official investigation. It was denied them, whereupon they demanded to see the prelate who had acted as Moderator on the occasion, Cardinal Dopfner. But he was not available, having gone to Capri for a long week-end.

When they succeeded in gaining an interview the Cardinal apologised, and then coolly asked them to resign their right to speak. That was naturally turned down, whereupon the Cardinal promised to read aloud a summary of the speeches they had prepared. But those who gathered in the Council Hall could hardly recognise the versions they heard. They had been considerably shortened, their meaning was confused and, in some cases, falsified. Then, after the manner of their kind, the objectors gave up, defeated by their own lethargy-or was it by the shifts and persistence of those who had come to the Council with a set purpose and a pattern that was being repeated again and again throughout the sessions?

On a day late in October the attention of the Council was concentrated on a figure who rose to speak. He was Alfredo Cardinal Ottaviani, one of the ablest members of the Curia, who carried with him a sense of the great days of Pius XII, on which account he was respected by some, and feared or disliked by others. Some shrank from his glance, which, said his enemies, was due to his possessing the evil eye. His stare could indeed be disconcerting, since he had been born in the poverty-stricken Trastevere quarter, where an eye disease, which had raged unattended, had afflicted many, and now, at seventy odd years, he was nearly blind.

When he rose the progressives in the Council exchanged meaning looks. They knew what was coming. He was about to criticise the new form of the Mass, the work of Monsignor Annibale Bugnini (which we propose to look at a little more closely later).

Acclaimed by the progressives, and deplored by the traditionalists as a fatal innovation, it had brought about a deeper rift within the Council than any other topic.

There was no doubt in anyone's mind as to the side on which Ottaviani would be ranged, and his first words made that clear: Are we seeking to stir up wonder, perhaps scandal, among the Christian people, by introducing changes in so venerable a rite, that has been approved by so many centuries, and is now so familiar? The rite of Holy Mass should not be treated as if it were a piece of cloth to be refashioned according to the whim of each generation....

The time limit for speakers was ten minutes. The finger of Cardinal Alfrink, who had charge of the proceedings, was on the warning bell. This speaker was over earnest, and what he had to say was displeasing to many. The ten minutes passed. The bell rang, and Cardinal Alfrink signalled to a technician who switched off the microphone. Ottaviani confirmed what had happened by tapping the instrument. Then, totally humiliated, he stumbled back to his seat, feeling with his hands and knocking against the woodwork as he went. There were those among the Council Fathers who sniggered. Others clapped.

These pages are not intended to be concerned with Papal authority. But it has to be dealt with, however briefly, as those who may still doubt the secret society involvement, and the degree of power with which I have invested it, may point to the fact that one of their most extreme claims, 'The Papacy will fall,' has not been borne out. For the Papacy is still in existence.

In existence, yes. But it has yielded place to a spirit of collectivism that would never have been credited in the days when Peter and his successors, by virtue of the authority vested in Peter by Christ, were known to have been given supreme jurisdiction over the Church.

Even while the Council was still in session many of its members, led by the Bishop of Baltimore, were negating the doctrine of Papal infallibility which, by relating specifically to faith and morals, was much more restricted than many think; and similar moves elsewhere led to its replacement by a new and clumsy definition-the Episcopal Collegiality of the Bishops.

Such a delegation of authority has now come about. More responsibility has passed to the Bishops, and the general acceptance of such a change has been followed by a corresponding decline in the Papal monopoly of power.

That may be no more than a first step towards the fulfilment of the confident boast: 'The Papacy will fall.'

7.

Annibale Bugnini, created Titular Archbishop of Dioclentiana by Paul VI in 1972, had every reason to be pleased. His life-long service to the Church in the field of liturgical studies and reform had been rewarded. He was now, as Secretary to the Commission for the implementation of the Constitution on the Liturgy, a key figure in the revolution which had been pending for the past thirteen years. Even before the opening of the Second Vatican Council he had been bidding fair to play a decisive part in the future of the Church, much of which hinged upon the Mass, for which he had compiled new rites and a new order as a sign of further progress to come.'

His work entailed a reform of liturgical books and the transition from Latin to the vernacular, all to be achieved by easy stages that would not alarm the unsuspecting. The imposition of new and different rules was being accomplished so successfully that Cardinal Villot, one of their promulgators, could state that no fewer than a hundred and fifty changes were, after only twelve months, already in circulation; while as to the outdated stipulation that 'the use of Latin will be kept in the Latin rites,' Mass was already being said in thirty-six dialects, in patois, even in a kind of everyday slang.

Bugnini had, in fact, with the approval of Paul VI, put into practice Luther's programme, in which it had been recognised that 'when the Mass is destroyed, the Papacy will have been toppled, for the Papacy leans on the Mass as on a rock.' It was true that an orthodox opponent, Dietrich von Hildebrand, had called Bugnini 'the evil spirit of liturgical reform.' But no such consideration figured in the Archbishop's mind as, on a day in 1975, he left a conference room where he had attended a meeting of one of the Commissions where he had a voice, and started to climb a staircase. Suddenly he stopped. His hands, which should have been carrying a brief case, were empty. The case, containing many of his papers, had been left in the conference room. Never one to hurry, for he was a heavy man and needed exercise, he now fairly ran back and cast his eye over the chairs and tables. The brief case was nowhere to be seen.

As soon as the meeting broke up, a Dominican friar had gone in to restore the room to order.

He soon noticed the brief case, and had opened it in the hope of finding the name of its owner. He put aside the documents relating to the Commission, and had then come upon a folder that contained letters.

Sure enough, there was the name of the person to whom they had been sent, but-and the Dominican gasped-the mode of address was not to His Grace or to the Most Reverend Annibale Bugnini, Archbishop of Dioclentiana, but to Brother Bugnini, while the signatures and place of origin showed that they came from the dignitaries of secret societies in Rome.

Pope Paul VI who was, of course, tarred with the same brush as Bugnini, promptly took steps to prevent the scandal spreading, and to smooth over the dismay of those progressives who, innocent of guile, had no opinion other than that dictated by the media. Bugnini should have been removed, or at least taken to task. But he was, instead, for the sake of appearances, appointed Apostolic Pro Nuncio in Iran, a post where there was little or no call for diplomatic embellishment since the Shah's government had no time for any Western religion, and where the priest who was unfortunate enough to be banished there, though only for a time, found his function as limited as his surroundings, which consisted of scanty furniture in two rooms in an otherwise empty house.

The unmasking of Bugnini was carried a step further when the Italian writer, Tito Casini, who was troubled over the changes in the Church, made it known in The Smoke of Satan, a novel that was published in April 1976. Then came the expected denials and evasions. A Vatican source declared that the reasons for

Bugnini's removal had to remain secret though, it was admitted, the motives that prompted, it had been 'more than convincing.' Le Figaro issued a denial of any secret society connection on Bugnini's behalf. The Catholic Information Office belied its title by professing total ignorance of the case. Archbishop Bugnini more than once denied any secret society affiliation. All of which appears very futile since the Italian Register reveals that he joined one of the societies on April the 23rd, 1963, and that his code name was Buan.

8.

On the 8th day of December, 1965, Pope Paul confronted the assembled Bishops, raised both arms high in the air, and announced: 'In the name of Our Lord Jesus Christ, go in peace.'

The Second Vatican Council was over; and those who heard Pope Paul gave vent to the feelings of victory, or defeat, that had sprung up among them during the meetings.

The conservatives were resentful, indignant, and hinted of a counter-offensive that was never to be mounted. They agreed among themselves that the Church's progress had been halted by a move that was both unwise and unnecessary. One of their spokesmen, Cardinal Siri, spoke of resistance. 'We are not going to be bound by these decrees;' but the decrees were, in fact, implemented, as Pope Paul had promised, to the growing bewilderment of Catholics for whom the Church, now a prey to novelties and disorders, had lost its note of authority.

The liberals or progressives, secure in having brought the designs of the secret societies to a successful conclusion, were exultant. The Council, said the Swiss theologian Hans Kung, had more than fulfilled the dreams of the *avant-garde*. The entire world of religion was now permeated by its influence, and no member of the Council 'would go back home as he had come.' 'I myself,' he continued, 'never expected so many bold and explicit statements from the Bishops on the Council floor.'

In a similar mood the Dominican Yves Congar, a life-long Left-winger, announced that past failures in the Church had been brought about by its being imbued with the spirit of Latin-Western culture. But that culture, he was glad to announce, had had its day.

The most extreme reformer, Cardinal Suenens, executed a mental war-dance of triumph. He looked back to the Council of Milan, held in 313, by which the Emperor Constantine gave complete toleration to Christians, and made their faith equal to what, until then, had been the official State religion. That decree had always been a landmark in Church history. But now the Belgian primate who was known to his fellow conspirators as Lesu, could throw all such epoch-making reminders overboard. He was on the winning side. He bid defiance to those who differed from him. 'The age of Constantine is over!' Moreover, he claimed he would be able to draw up an impressive list of theses that, having been taught in Rome yesterday, had been believed, but at which the Council Fathers had snapped their fingers.

These danger signs were recognised by Malachi Martin, formerly a Jesuit and Professor at the Pontifical Biblical Institute in Rome. 'Well before the year 2,000,' he said, there will no longer be a religious institute recognisable as the Roman Catholic and Apostolic Church of today.... There will be no centralised control, no uniformity in teaching, no universality in practice of worship, prayer, sacrifice, and priesthood.'

Can one detect the first signs of this in the Anglican-Roman Catholic International Commission's report published in March, 1982?

A more precise assessment of the post-Conciliar period, than that made by Malachi Martin, appeared in the *American Flag Committee Newsletter*, 1967. Commenting on the 'most marked and rapid deterioration in the Vatican's anti-Bolshevik resolve' since the time of Pius XII, it goes on to say that in less than a decade the Church has been transformed 'from an implacable foe of Communism into an active and quite powerful advocate of co-existence both with Moscow and Red China. At the same time, revolutionary changes in its centuries-long teachings have moved Rome closer and closer, not to traditional Protestantism as many Catholic laymen suppose, but to that humanistic neo-paganism of the National and World Council of Churches.'

But if the Council accomplished nothing else, it enabled the caterers to flourish. For some half-a-million cups of coffee were disposed of at the bars.

Part Four

The Devil has recovered his citizenship rights in the Republic of culture.

Giovanni Papini.

Publicity flared to its maximum coverage when it was announced, in the summer of 1965, that Pope Paul would visit New York later that year in order to address the United Nations Assembly. It was heralded as an event of the utmost importance that would surely bring results that could not be lost upon the world; but there was also some speculation as to why non-Catholic, and even anti-Catholic quarters, were giving rise to much the same bursts of excitement that had marked the election of John XXIII.

Could it be that the same power was pulling wires, behind the scenes, to influence the tone of the Press, radio, and television? We have already assessed, to some extent, the character and the leanings of Paul VI. Let us now glance at the formation and the make-up of the United Nations.

It was primarily Communist in tone, its charter, signed in 1943, being based upon the Constitution of Soviet Russia, while its purpose and principles were decided at a conference of Foreign Ministers held in Moscow.

The secretaries of the United Nations' Security Council, between the years 1946 and 1962, were Arkady Sobelov and Eugeny Kiselev, both Communists. A leading figure of the United Nations' Educational, Scientific, and Cultural Organization

(U.N.E.S.C.O.) was Vladimir Mailmovsky, Communist. The chief secretary for U.N.E.S.C.O. was Madame Jegalova, Communist; while the President, Vice-President, and nine judges of the 'World Court' were all Communists.

Yet these were typical of the people on whom Paul VI lavished praise, and to whom he looked for the salvation of the world; while the Press and radio, subject to the same international control as the United Nations, continues to speak of that body as being worthy of respect.

Posing as strictly neutral, and with the declared intention of promoting world peace, it soon showed a definite bias in favour of Communist-inspired guerrilla movements whose object, in several parts of the world, was the overthrow of established governments. This was done under the guise of liberating people from oppression; but the ultimate design of the Assembly, then as now, was to set up a totalitarian system in which national sovereignty and cultures would disappear.

Incidental to this, as was made plain by the secondary social and economic organisations that sprang from the Assembly, would be a virtual censorship whose voice was predominantly atheist.

For it had been noted that the more orthodox countries such as Italy, Austria, Spain, Portugal, and Ireland, were excluded from the Assembly's original foundation; whereas Bolshevist Russia, from its permanent seat on the Security Council, possessed a veto that could reduce the decisions of the Assembly to a mere expression of words, without effect; a judgment that may fairly be passed on all the deliberations of the United Nations from the day of its founding to the present.

More concrete evidence for these strictures may be adduced when we look at the record of a professional criminal who came to occupy a leading place, by way of the United Nations, in European life. He was Meyer Genoch Moisevitch Vallakh, or Wallach, who, before 'the 1914 war, emerged from the stormy background of Russian political life as a 'wanted' figure who found it safer, and more rewarding, to extend his activities to countries that were, so far, less disturbed.

Working under a variety of names, including Buchmann, Maxim Harryson, Ludwig Nietz, David Mordecai, and Finkelstein, he came into the limelight in Paris in 1908, when he took a hand in robbing the Tiflis Bank of two hundred and fifty thousand roubles. He was deported, but soon afterwards was in trouble again for dealing in stolen banknotes.

His chance came in 1917, when the Russian Revolution brought him and his kind to the surface. Now, under the respectable pseudonym of Maxim Litvinoff, he became Soviet Commissioner for Foreign Affairs. His next step was to the Presidency of the Council of the League of Nations. He then arrived in London as Soviet ambassador to the Court of St. James, and as such became a familiar and influential figure in royal and diplomatic circles.

As further evidence of the downward slide in our public and political affairs, it may be noted that the first Secretary-General of the United Nations was Alger Hiss, who had been convicted of perjury in the American courts. He took a prominent part in shaping the United Nations' Charter on Russian-Communist lines.

These considerations, however, did not weigh heavily with the faithful, who thought that the Pope's address and appearance, before a world audience, would be a golden opportunity for the advancement of Papal teaching. It would burst upon the doubting and insecure world with a certainty that it had never before experienced. Many listeners, for the first time in their lives, would be brought face to face with the reality of religion. It was only the Church that had anything really important to say, that could add spiritual significance to the routine of daily life.

Some half-a-century before, Pius X had issued directions and indicated guide-lines that were everywhere and at all times relevant. But his audience had been as necessarily limited as his means to make himself heard. Now it was for Pope Paul to echo the words of his predecessor, but this time to an almost universal congregation that could be reached through the medium of the United Nations.

Pius had said: 'There is no need for me to point out that the advent of world democracy can have no relevancy to the work of the Church in the world ... the reform of civilisation is essentially a religious task, for true civilisation pre-supposes a moral foundation, and there can be no morally based foundation without true religion... this is a truth which can be demonstrated from the evidence of history.'

But Pope Paul had no intention of endorsing what Pius had said. For instead of a religious leader speaking on October 4th, 1965, it might have been a disciple of Jean Jacques Rousseau holding forth on the deification of human nature that, finding expression in the declaration of the Rights of Man on August 12th, 1789, ushered in the French Revolution.

The Rights of Man, that were enthusiastically defined as being vested in Liberty, Equality, and Fraternity, led to the Cult of Man and man's elevation in place of God; from which it followed that all religious forms, and institutions such as rulership, family life, and the holding of private property, were denigrated as being parts of the old order that was on the point of passing.

When the effects of the Second Vatican Council became apparent, Doctor Rudolf Gruber, Bishop of Regensburg, was led to observe that the main ideas of the French Revolution, 'which represents an important element in Lucifer's plan,' were being adopted in many spheres of Catholicism. And Pope Paul, speaking direct to a battery of microphones that carried to the world, gave ample evidence of this.

He made no reference to spiritual claims or the importance of religion. 'Behold the day we have awaited for centuries.... This is the ideal that mankind has dreamt of in its journey through history.... We would venture to call it the world's greatest hope.... It is your task here,' he told the members of the Assembly, 'to proclaim the basic rights and duties of Man.... We are conscious that you are the interpreters of all that is permanent in human wisdom; we could almost say of its sacred character.'

Man had now come of age, and was qualified to live by a philosophic-morality that, owing nothing to authority, was created by himself. The United Nations, destined to play the leading role in the world, was 'the last hope of mankind.' So it was to secular structures that man must look for the stability and redemption of humanity; in a word, to himself; sentiments that would not have been out of place in the committee rooms of the French Revolution; sentiments that no one would have thought to hear expressed by a Pope, void as they were of any reference to the claims and traditional message of the Church.

That this was understood and appreciated was shown by the reception accorded him at the close of his address, by those of a certain political persuasion who made up by far the greater part of his live audience. He was surrounded by back-slapping and handshaking representatives of Russia, China, and the Soviet satellite States. He arranged for further meetings, which proved to be four in all, with the Soviet Foreign Minister Gromyko (real name Katz), and his wife. There were congratulations from Nikolai Podgorny, member of the Politburo, and warm exchanges with Arthur Goldberg, a prominent member of the Communist Party.

Pope Paul had opened up the world of religion to its old and inveterate enemies, the champions of social reform who denied revelation. 'Dialogue' was now much in fashion, and the prospect of Moscow and the Vatican entering into talks was taken for granted. The world's leading churchman had propagated the social gospel, so dear to the heart of revolutionaries, without a single reference to the religious doctrines that they found pernicious. Differences between the two sides were not so deep-seated and final as had once been thought. The Pope, and those who clustered about him sometimes with two-handed clasps, could henceforth be allies.

It now remained to round off a truly historic visit with an initiatory rite that would put the seal on this newly admitted realisation.

2.

'Behold, thy King is coming to thee, humbly riding on an ass.' So wrote St. Matthew (21.5) on Christ's entry into Jerusalem.

But it was not thus that Christ's representative rode along Broadway. Pope Paul travelled in a seven-passenger Lincoln convertible, through a forest of flags and bunting, with a police escort on motor cycles, and thousands more police lining the way and restraining crowds that were uncertain whether to stand, kneel, or bow their heads in expectation of a blessing, and whether to wave or raise an arm in salute; with two spotter helicopters buzzing and circling overhead, sirens ~ blowing, and on nearly every building fluorescent lighting that unnecessarily vied with the daylight, and the United Nations' Plaza Building spelling out 'welcome, Pope Paul VI.'

This followed upon a question that Cardinal Vagnozzi, the Apostolic-delegate in New York, put to Pope Paul. What was to be the next goal of his visit?

The Meditation Room in the United Nations' building, Paul told him.

The Cardinal was surprised, shocked. He had good reason for affirming that the Holy Father couldn't go there.

But he went.

The room, with two others of its kind, one at Wainwright House, Stuyvesant Avenue, Rye, New York, and the other in the United States Capitol, represented the early stage of a scheme the fulfilment of which would be marked (in concrete form) by the erection of what was called the Temple of Understanding, on fifty acres of ground along the banks of the Potomac in Washington, D.C.

It was part of a design to form one inter-religious world body on the part of a certain Mrs. Judith Dickerman Hollister, who revealed an anti-traditional, pro-mysterious bias by becoming a Shinto. As such, she believed the Japanese myth that two divine universal parents descended upon an island that was made of drops of salt. There the god-mother gave birth to other islands, with mountains and rivers, and finally to a whole galaxy of gods. After that astonishing feat the lady withdrew from her sea-girt home and was seen no more.

Thus armed with an air of mystery, a suggestion of interior enlightenment, and an eccentric bearing, Mrs. Hollister found an enthusiastic supporter in the President's wife, Eleanor Roosevelt, whom some of her intimates rated as being somewhat below the mentally normal.

From that it needed but a step to secure the backing of the United States Government, while John D. Rockefeller, and several of his associates in the Communist front- that he founded, contributed to what was called the Spiritual United Nations. Another pro-Communist millionaire, Marshall Field, who has already been noted as a patron of the anarchist Saul David Alinsky, helped to pay for the decoration of the room. The Ford Foundation also gave financial encouragement.

A carefully edited bulletin, that supposedly dealt with the meaning and purpose of the room, was produced by the Lucis Press, which issues printed matter for the United Nations. The suspicious may find food for thought in the fact that this publishing company, when it started in the early part of this century, was known as the Lucifer Press. It now functions at 3 Whitehall Court, London, S.W.1.

That title might well have been retained when dealing with Mrs. Hollister's creation, for the room (and this explains the shock felt by Cardinal Vagnozzi) was a centre of the Illuminati, given over to the cult of the all-seeing Eye that under a system of allegories and veiled secrets, as translated by the Masters of Wisdom, was dedicated to the service of pagan cults; and the obliteration of Christian in favour of humanistic beliefs.

3.

Two doors, each fitted with tinted glass panels, lead into the room. A guard stands outside, and another is stationed just inside the door. The entrant encounters semi-darkness, and a quiet into which one's footsteps are absorbed by a thick blue rug on the floor. An arched inner way, still overhung by a sense of night-like stillness, opens out into a space some thirty feet long, wedge-shaped, windowless, and with a solitary yellow light, apparently beamed from nowhere, shimmering on the surface of an altar that stands in the centre, a waist-high block of crystalline iron ore that is known to weigh between six and seven tons.

Blue rugs are spread over the floor, that is elsewhere paved with blue-grey lengths of slate. At the far end of the room, where the dimness melts into total shadow, there is a low railing beyond which only the privileged are allowed to pass.

The fresco-mural, more than eight feet high and some two feet smaller in width, is played upon by a light directed from the top. Framed in a steel panel, it appears to be an apparently meaningless cluster of blue, grey, white, brown, and yellow geometrical designs. But to those versed in esoteric understanding the crescents and triangles present a definite form that takes shape, in the centre and outer circle of the mural, as the Illuminati Eye.

Main attention is not, however, focused upon the mural but on the altar, that is dedicated to the 'faceless one,' and from which an air of brooding mystery, prevalent in the room, appears to radiate. And as one's senses respond it is realised that other shaded lights, concealed in a suspended ceiling that matches the size of the room, add to the sombre impression conveyed by the altar beam.

Pope Paul, at the end of his mission, was presented with a model of the then prospective Temple of Understanding. The Masters extended a similar welcome to Cardinal Suenens, who later visited the Meditation Room; and in return representatives of the Temple were received at the Vatican.

The underlying purpose of the Temple was plainly revealed by its plan, with the all-seeing Eye, faceted like a diamond in the central dome of the building, reflecting the rays of the sun through wings that represented six world faiths-Buddhism, Hinduism, Islam, Judaism, Confucianism, and Christianity.

The same symbolism figured at a banquet attended by some five hundred supporters of syncretism at the Waldorf Astor, where a little scene was enacted when a child, holding aloft the model of an egg, was presented to the president of the Temple, the same Mrs. Dickerman Hollister. She tapped the egg with a wand, and the shell dropped away to reveal a tree with six golden branches.

Before leaving America Pope Paul, to press home his voluntary renunciation of spiritual authority, made a show of divesting himself of the Church's reminders and insignia. He gave the Papal ring of diamonds and rubies, and his pectoral cross of diamonds and emeralds-the two containing four hundred and four diamonds, one hundred and forty-five emeralds, and twenty rubies-to the Buddhist U Thant, then Secretary-General of the United Nations.

A jeweller had estimated that the jewels alone, apart from their traditional value, were worth more than a hundred thousand dollars. They were swept up at an auction for sixty-four thousand dollars, after which the successful buyer sold them to a Mr. David Morton of Orono, Minnesota.

Some items of this Papal jewellery were next seen decking the person of a female performer who appeared in the Carson television night-show.'

The ring 'and the cross continued to go the round of dealers, auction rooms, and superior junk shops, and were last heard of among the articles offered for sale at a market in Geneva.

This abnegation followed Pope Paul's public show of giving up the tiara, the triple crown that denotes the Trinity, the authority, and the spiritual powers of the Church. The crown was presented to a Pope at the time of his coronation with the words: 'Receive this tiara adorned with three crowns and know that you are the father of princes and of kings, guide of the world, and Vicar upon earth of Jesus Christ.'

Pope Paul let it be known that he was giving up the crown for the benefit of the poor of the world, a motive that was played up by the Press and that 'went down well' with the public. But he was giving up something that had never been his, in the first place, and so was not transferable. Moreover, one word from him would have caused all the world-wide missions and charitable organisations of the Church to open their purses for the poor. But instead, he made a theatrical gesture by discarding external signs of religious dignity which, as he and his kind well knew, was a minor step that, added to others of its kind, was part of the process of sapping the Church's internal significance.

He also made use of a sinister symbol, used by Satanists in the sixth century, that had been revived at the time of Vatican Two. This was a bent or broken cross on which was displayed a repulsive and distorted figure of Christ, which the black magicians and sorcerers of the Middle Ages had made use of to represent the Biblical term, 'Mark of the Beast.'

Yet not only Paul VI but his successors, the two John-Pauls, carried that object and held it up to be revered by crowds who had not the slightest idea that it stood for anti-Christ. Furthermore, this exhibition of a desiccated figure on a twisted stick was forbidden by Canon 1279, which condemned the usage of any sacred image that is not in keeping with the approved usage of the Church. That it was used for occult purposes may be seen in woodcuts shown in the Museum of Witchcraft in Bayonne, France.

Another disquieting feature of Pope Paul's visit to the United States was his appearance, at the Yankee Stadium in New York, wearing the Ephod, the ancient garment with breastplate of twelve stones, representing the twelve sons of Jacob, as worn by

Caiphas, the High Priest of the Sanhedrin, who called for the crucifixion of Christ.

As though not content with that quite unnecessary innovation, His Holiness continued to wear that non-Christian symbol on other occasions, including the Way of the Cross procession in Rome on March the 27th, 1964; at a ceremony in the Place d'Espagne, Rome, on December the 8th, 1964; the visit of Doctor Ramsay, Archbishop of Canterbury, to the Vatican in 1966; at a reception of parish priests in the Sistine Chapel; and at Castelgandolpho in the summer of 1970.

The tone of Pope Paul's address to the United Nations had given no little encouragement to the progressives, or Left-wing element, within the Church. For within a few days of Paul's return to Rome the Bishop of Cuernavaca, Mendes Arceo, was declaring that 'Marxism is necessary in order to realise God's kingdom at the present time;' while Pope Paul let it be known that Rome, in order to end an old enmity, was ready to take a new look at secret societies.

As part of that process, Monsignor Pezeril was entrusted with the task of negotiating with a governing body of those societies with a view to establishing friendly contact.

The retentive powers of those who write for the papers, like the memories of those who seriously regard them, are proverbially short. Yet because the Pope's speech in New York was well in keeping with the prevailing trend, it is not surprising to find that the cue he had given there was taken up, some time later, by the Vatican journal *L'Osservatore Romano*, which let it be known that the Church's traditional message had yielded place to a more unorthodox concept, by announcing:

'There are no true riches but Man.'

(The two interlaced triangles explain Lantoine's remarks that Satan is an equal and indispensable part of God, as seen when the picture is reversed. Simply translated, the motto means: 'What is above equals what is below.' It reveals a common occult idea that God-is both good and evil, and that Satan is part of him.)

Part Five

> *The veil covering the greatest deceit ever to have mystified the clergy and baffled the faithful, is doubtless beginning to be torn asunder.*
>
> Archbishop Marcel Lefebvre.

An observer of the Roman scene, Georges Virebeau,[13] tells how a feeling of surprise, that was near A consternation, spread through the Vatican one morning in 1976. Students in their cassocks, coloured purple, violet, or black, according to their nationality, stood about in groups, discussing the latest number of a journal, the *Borghese*. Some, the writer says, were actually perspiring with alarm; for although the morning was hot, the atmosphere engendered by what they read affected them more than the weather.

For the paper contained a detailed list of clerics, some holding the most exalted offices, who were said to be members of secret societies.

It was staggering news, for the doubtful head-shaking students were acquainted with Church law; and Canon Law 2335 expressly declared that a Catholic who joined any such society became excommunicate, ipso facto.

---

[13] In *Prélats et Francs-Maçons*. (Henri Coston, Paris, 1978.)

We have seen that the secret societies had, long ago, declared war on the Church, which they recognised as the one great obstacle barring their way to -world domination; and the Church responded by condemning the societies and making laws for her own protection. Canon 2335 was framed for that purpose, while Canon 2336 was concerned with disciplinary measures to be enforced against any cleric who might be inveigled into joining a society. In the case of a Bishop he would lose all juridical powers, and be barred from exercising priestly functions including ordination and consecrating.

That the Church considered the societies to be a most dangerous threat to its own existence is shown by the number of warnings and condemnations issued by the Vatican. What is usually regarded as the first official instance of this occurred under Pope Clement XII (1730-40), which stressed that belonging to any such society was incompatible with membership of the Church.

Eleven years later Benedict XIV confirmed this in the first Papal Bull directed against the societies. Pius VI and Pius VII followed suit, the last named being specially concerned with the threat posed by the Carbonari. Three subsequent Popes, Leo XII, Pius VIII, and Gregory VI added their weight to the strictures. A further condemnation came from Pius IX who, incidentally had to face the charge that he had descended from the Counts of Mastai-Feretti, who had almost certainly been involved with the societies. Leo XIII spoke of the plotters aiming to destroy from top to bottom the whole religious and social discipline born of Christian institutions,' and to replace belief in the supernatural spirit by a sort of second-hand Naturalism.

Just as the writings of Voltaire, Diderot, and Helvetius had opened up the way for the French Revolution, so the secret societies, said Pius X (1903-14) were working to destroy Catholicism in modern France.

So paramount was the danger to Benedict XV that not even the cares imposed by the 1914 war could drive it finally from his mind; while Pius XI reiterated that the secret societies derived much of their strength from the conspiracy of silence that has never ceased to surround them.

Although conducted largely behind the scenes, and therefore away from the public gaze, the struggle between the Church and the secret societies has been more bitter and prolonged than any international conflict; the reason being that it has turned, in great part, on *ideas*, on a mental and therefore a moral basis; and although not universally recognised, the moral outlook influences the whole nature of man more than any conflict for personal gain, territory, or positive power.

On one side was a religion that, its supporters claimed, rested on facts, the objective value of revealed truth, and a sacramental observance. On the other, a system grounded in humanitarian ideals in which all men, freed from the shackles or dogma and orthodoxy, could share, and on which they could agree. Truth, they said, is relative, hence the claims of objective and revealed truth are seen to be not only valueless, but fundamentally false.

So the struggle developed over the centuries, with those who accepted the atheism, Positivism, or materialism that reached its summit with the French Revolution, on one side; and the strictures uttered by various Popes, from Clement XII in the mid-eighteenth century to Pius XI who died in 1939, on the other.

The least condemnatory of those strictures referred to the societies as 'conspiracies of silence.'

The most damning called them 'synagogues of Satan.'

But not all their members regarded the Satanic connection as a stigma. This is how one of their principle archivists, Albert Lantoine, went out of his way to address Pius XII in August, 1943: Ì am pleased to say that we, possessed of a critical spirit, are servants of Satan. You defend truth, and are servants of God. The two masters complete each other, and need each other.

You would exterminate us. Be careful! The death of Satan will mark the agony of your God. You must accept the alliance with Satan, and admit that he completes God.'

The news in the *Borghese,* that so alarmed the students, came as the culmination of a fear that had lingered for some time among the more conservative elements in the Vatican. The exposure of

Archbishop Bugnini, at the time of the Second Vatican Council, had been shattering enough.

But the revelations in the *Borghese* were on a more considerable scale, and came perilously near to touching the very nerve of the Church.

It was known that enemy agents had long been nibbling at its fabric. But so long as Church discipline remained strong, it was difficult for the most ardent infiltrator to gain a footing in the priesthood. But the general relaxation and reforms that followed Pope John's Council opened doors by which agents entered not only seminaries but the Curia, the governing body of the Church.

Because some of those agents rose high in the Church, and became Cardinals and Bishops, many who might otherwise have been suspicious were deceived. The ecclesiastical titles, and the offices that went with them, were thought to be sufficient (though they were really only outward), safeguard. The hands of the manipulators were raised in blessing, and the faithful knelt.

The warnings against them that were issued went largely unheeded or fell stone dead against the historically impressive walls that bounded the Church. A Fifth Column exists within the clergy,' wrote Father Arrupe, Superior-General of the Jesuits, and is steadily working in favour of atheism.'

A similar theme was expressed by a number of theologians who came together in Geneva in 1976, as an International Committee of Defence of Catholic Doctrine. 'The presence of the enemies of the Church, in the internal structure of the Church, forms a part of the mystery of iniquity and should be unmasked.'

But so far those fears had taken no more tangible shape than to unsettle the minds of students, who felt their future might be disturbed by the revelations that produced little or no effect among their superiors and instructors in the Vatican. The usual inquiry was ordered (by some of the churchmen who had been named as guilty) with the declared object of tracing the source of the rumours. But nothing happened; and neither did one of those who had been implicated ever issue a downright or straightforward denial.

The *Borghese* article claimed to have a detailed list of conspirators who had penetrated into the Church, together with dates, numbers, and code names. These allegations were answered by a writer in *L'Aurora*, M. Jacques Ploncard, who asserted that no prelate had been affiliated with a secret society since the time of Charles X, the last of the Bourbons who ascended the throne in 1824, and was driven out by the revolution of 1830.

This was palpably false, as was proved by determined investigators who carried the attack into enemy territory. By one means or another, sometimes posing as members of the Government, they gained access to the Italian Register of Secret Societies, and drew up a much longer and more impressive list than that published in the *Borghese*.

The particulars that follow are those of Cardinals, Archbishops, and Bishops who, as alleged by those who examined it, figure in the Register. Some have died since the list was drawn up-at one time it was said to have included one hundred and twenty-five prelates. Some of the offices have changed hands.

But the names and ecclesiastical titles, with the dates on which they were initiated into a society, and their secret code names, must call for serious consideration, except from those Catholics who blindly follow the rules, who hang upon the words of a priest, and who think it part of their faith to see no stain upon the Church.

It may be noted that the code name often incorporates the first two letters of the cleric's name.

2.

- **Agostino, Cardinal Casaroli.** Secretary of State. Prefect of the Sacred Congregation of Public Affairs, and of the Sacred Congregation of Bishops, and of the Pontifical Commission for the Revision of Canon Law. Member of the Commission for Russia and of the Commission for Latin America. The most influential prelate in the Vatican after the Pope, whose place he takes during the absence of the latter. He is known as the 'Kissinger of Vatican diplomacy.' Initiated into a secret society September 28th, 1957. Secret code name Casa.

- **Leon Joseph, Cardinal Suenens.** Primate of Belgium. Member of the Pontifical Commission for the Revision of Canon Law. Was active in the Sacred Congregation of Propaganda Fide, the Sacred Congregation of Rites and Ceremonies, and the Sacred Congregation of Seminaries and University Studies. He was a delegate and Moderator of the Second Vatican Council, and he has been associated with Protestant Pentecostalism, that reduces people to revivalist hysteria. Initiated June 15th, 1967. Code name Lesu.

- **Jean, Cardinal Villot.** He was Secretary of State to Paul VI, and Camerlengo (the Chamberlain who takes over affairs at the Vatican on the death of a Pope). Prefect of the Sacred Congregation for Religious and Secular. Institutes, and administrator of the Patrimony of the Holy See. He came of a family which has produced over the last two hundred years, from father to son, Grand Masters of secret societies including the Rosicrucians. Being aware that this had become known, he strenuously denied that he was associated in any way with such societies. One of his denials was contained in a letter, dated October 31st, 1976, sent from the Vatican by way of the Papal Nunciature in Paris, to the Director of *Lectures Françaises,* a monthly publication. It ran: 'Having noticed that in your review of September 1976, you referred to Cardinal Villot as a member of a secret society, Cardinal Villot declares in the most formal fashion that he has never had, at any moment in his life, the least connection with any secret society. He adheres closely to the condemnations imposed by the Sovereign Pontiffs. Cardinal Villot begs the Director of *Lectures Françaises* to publish this denial in a future issue, and thanks him in advance.' One cannot help wondering how Cardinal Villot, who appears to have been afflicted with an unusually short memory, managed to fulfil his office as Secretary of State. For records show that he was initiated into a secret society on August 6th, 1966, and that in the hope of avoiding identification he was given two code names, Jeani and Zurigo.

➢ **Achille, Cardinal Lienart.** Bishop of Lille. He was formerly a captain in the French Army, and a life-long ultra-Liberal. He led the progressive forces at the Second Vatican Council, on which account it was said that 'his ideas were redder than his robes.' Shortly before his death he startled those in the room by suddenly exclaiming: 'Humanly speaking, the Church is dead.' Initiated October 15th, 1912. Code name could not be verified.

➢ **Ugo, Cardinal Poletti.** Vicar-General of the diocese of Rome, and so controller of all the clergy in the city. Member of the Sacred Congregation of Sacraments and of Divine Worship. President of Pontifical Works, and of the Liturgical Academy. Archpriest of the Patriarchal Basilica of the Lateran. Initiated February 17th, 1969. Code name Upo.

➢ **Franco, Cardinal Biffi.** Head of the St. John Lateran Pontifical University. Initiated August 15th, 1969. Code name Bifra.

- **Michele, Cardinal Pellegrino**. Archbishop of Turin where the Holy Shroud is kept: Initiated May 2nd, 1960. Code name Palmi.
- **Sebastiano, Cardinal Baggio**. Prefect of the Sacred Congregation of Bishops. Initiated August 15th, 1957. Code name Seba.
- **Pasquale, Cardinal Macchi**. Prelate of Honour and secretary to Paul VI. After being excommunicated for heresy, he was reinstated by Cardinal Villot. Initiated April 23rd, 1958. Code name Mapa.
- **Salvatore, Cardinal Pappalardo**. Archbishop of Palermo, Sicily. Initiated May 6th, 1943. Code name Salpo.
- **Cardinal Garrone**. Prefect of the Congregation for Catholic Education. He brazenly let it be known that he was a member of a secret society, but he was neither removed nor publicly reproved. Date of initiation and code name could not be verified.
- **Archbishop Annibale Bugnini**. Consultant in the Sacred Congregation of Propagation of the Faith, and in the Sacred Congregation of Holy Rites. The story of his unmasking during the Second Vatican Council has been told. Died July 3rd, 1982. Initiated April 23rd, 1963. Code name Buan.
- **Archbishop Giovanni Benelli**. Archbishop of Florence. He secured the appointment of Cardinal Villot as Secretary of State in place of the orthodox Cardinal Cicognani. Date of initiation and code name could not be verified.
- **Archbishop Mario Brini**. Consultor of the Pontifical Commission for the Revision of Canon Law. Secretary of the Sacred Congregation for Eastern Churches, and a member of the Pontifical Commission for Russia. Initiated July 13th, 1969. Code name Mabri.
- **Bishop Michele Buro**. Prelate of the Pontifical Commission to Latin America. Initiated March 21st, 1969. Code name Bumi.

- **Bishop Fiorenzo Angelini**. Titular Bishop of Massene, Greece. Delegate of the Cardinal-Vicar of Rome for Hospitals. Initiated October 14th, 1957. Code name could not be verified.

- **Monsignor Mario Rizzi**. Prelate of Honour to the Holy Father. He was responsible for discarding certain Canon Laws which formed part of the foundation of the Church from Apostolic times. Initiated September 16th, 1969. Code name Mari or Monmari.

- **Monsignor Pio Vito Pinto**. Attache of Secretary of State, and Notary of the Second Section of the Supreme Tribunal and of the Apostolic Segnatura. He is listed as a very important person among the societies. Initiated April 2nd, 1970. Code name Pimpi.

- **Monsignor Francesco Marchisano**. Prelate of Honour to the Holy Father. Secretary of the Congregation for Catholic Education. Initiated February 14th, 1961. Code name Frama.

- **Aurelio Sabattani**. Archbishop of Giustiniana, Milan Province, Italy. First Secretary of the Supreme Apostolic Segnatura. Initiated June 22nd, 1969. Code name Asa.

- **Abino Mensa**. Archbishop of Vercelli, Piedmont, Italy. Initiated July 23rd, 1969. Code name Mena.

- **Enzio D'Antonio**. Archbishop of Trivento. Initiated June 21st, 1969. Code name could not be verified.

- **Alessandro Gottardi**. Archbishop of Trento, Italy. He controls candidates who are likely to be raised to the dignity of Cardinal. He is addressed as 'Doctor' at secret society meetings. Initiated June 13th, 1959. Code name Algo.

- **Antonio Travia**. Titular Bishop of Termini Imerese. He is the head of Catholic schools. Initiated September 15th, 1967. Code name Atra.

- **Giuseppe Mario Sensi**. Titular Bishop of Sardi, Asia Minor. Papal Nuncio to Portugal. Initiated November 2nd, 1967. Code name Gimase.

- Francesco Salerno. Bishop Prefect. Initiated May 4th, 1962. Code name Safra.
- Antonio Mazza. Titular Bishop of Velia. Initiated April 14th, 1971. Code name Manu.
- Mario Schierano. Titular Bishop of Acrida, Cosenza Province, Italy. Chief Military Chaplain of the Italian Armed Forces. Initiated July 3rd, 1959. Code name Maschi.
- Luigi Maverna. Bishop of Chiavari, Genoa, Italy. Initiated June 3rd, 1968. Code name Luma.
- Aldo Del Monte. Bishop of Novara, Piedmont, Italy. Initiated August 25th, 1969. Code name Adelmo.
- Marcello Morganta. Bishop of Ascoli, Piceno, in East Italy. Initiated July 22nd, 1955. Code name Morma.
- Luigi Bettazzi. Bishop of Lyrea, Italy. Initiated May 11th, 1966. Code name Lube.
- Gaetano Bonicelli. Bishop of Albano, Italy. Initiated May 12th, 1959. Code name Boga.
- Salvatore Baldassarri. Bishop of Ravenna, Italy. Initiated February 17th, 1958. Code name Balsa.
- Vito Gemmiti. Member of the Sacred Congregation of Bishops. Initiated March 25th, 1968. Code name Vige.
- Pier Luigi Mazzoni. Member of the Sacred Congregation of Bishops. Initiated September 14th, 1959. Code name Pilum.
- Ernesto Basadonna. Prelate of Milan. Initiated September 14th, 1963. Code name Base.
- Mario Bicarelli. Prelate of Vicenza, Italy. Initiated September 23rd, 1964. Code name Bima.
- Salvatore Marsili. Abbot of the Order of St. Benedict of Finalpia, near Modena, Italy. Initiated July 2nd, 1963. Code name Salma.

- **Annibale Ilari**. Abbot of Sua Santita. Initiated March 16th, 1969. Code name Ila.
- **Franco Gualdrini**. Rector of Capri. Initiated May 22nd, 1961. Code name Grefra.
- **Lino Lozza**. Chancellor of the Rome Academy of St. Thomas Aquinas. Initiated July 23rd, 1969. Code name Loli.
- **Daimazio Mongillo**. Professor of Dominican Moral Theology, Holy Angels Institute, Rome. Initiated February 16th, 1969. Code name Monda.
- **Flaminio Cerruti**. Chief of the Office of University of Congregation Studies. Initiated April 2nd, 1960.
- **Enrico Chiavacci**. Professor of Morals at the University of Florence. Initiated July 2nd, 1970. Code name Chie.
- **Carmelo Nigro**. Rector of the Seminary Pontifical of Major Studies. Initiated December 21st, 1970. Code name Carni.
- **Carlo Graziani**. Rector of the Minor Seminary of the Vatican. Initiated July 23rd, 1961. Code name Graca.
- **Luigi Belloli**. Rector of the Lombardy Seminary. Initiated April 6th, 1958. Code name Bella.
- **Virgilio Noe**. Head of the Sacred Congregation of Divine Worship. Initiated April 3rd, 1961. Code name Vino.
- **Dino Monduzzi**. Regent to the Prefect of the Pontifical House. Initiated March 11th, 1967. Code name Mondi.
- **Vittorio Palistra**. Legal Counsel to the Sacred Rota of the Vatican State. Initiated May 6th, 1943. Code name Pavi.
- **Giuseppe Ferraioli**. Member of the Sacred Congregation of Public Affairs of the Church. Initiated November 24th, 1969. Code name Gife.
- **Alberto Bovone**. Substitute-Secretary of the Sacred Office. Initiated April 30th, 1967.
- **Terzo Nattelino**. Vice-Prefect of the Archives of Secretariat of the Vatican. Initiated June 17th, 1957. Code name Nate.

- **Georgio Vale**. Priest official of the Rome diocese. Initiated February 21st, 1971. Code name Vagi.
- **Dante Balboni**. Assistant to the Vatican Pontifical Commission for Biblical Studies. Initiated July 23rd, 1968. Code name Balda.
- **Vittorio Trocchi**. Secretary for Catholic Laity in Consistory of the Vatican State Consultations. Initiated July 12th, 1962. Code name Trovi.
- **Piero Vergari**. Head Protocol Officer of the Vatican State Segnatura. He controls Canon Law changes. Initiated December 14th, 1970. Code name Pive.
- **Dante Pasquinelli**. Member of the Council of the Nuncio to Madrid. Initiated January 12th, 1969. Code name Pada.
- **Mario Pimpo**. Vicar of the Office of General Affairs. Initiated March 15th, 1970. Code name Pima.
- **Igino Rogger**. Officer in the diocese of Rome. Initiated April 16th, 1968. Code name Igno.
- **Pietro Rossano**. Member of the Sacred Congregation of nonChristian Studies. Initiated February 12th, 1968. Code name Piro.
- **Francesco Santangelo**. Substitute-General of Defence Legal Council. Initiated November 12th, 1970. Code name Frasa.
- **Gaetano Scanagatta**. Member of the Commission of Pompeii and Loreto. Initiated September 23rd, 1971. Code name Gasca.
- **Pio Laghi**. Apostolic Delegate to Argentina. Initiated August 24th, 1969. Code name Lapi.
- **Pietro Santini**. Vice-Official of the Tribunal of the Vicariate of the Vatican. Initiated August 23rd, 1964. Code name Sapa.

- **Domenico Semproni.** Member of the Tribunal of the. Vicariate of the Vatican. Initiated April 16th, 1960. Code name Dose.
- **Angelo Lanzoni.** Chief of the Office of Secretariat of State. Initiated September 24th, 1956. Code name Lana.
- **Giovanni Lajola.** Member of the Council of Public Affairs of the Church. Initiated July 27th, 1970. Code name Lagi.
- **Venerio Mazzi.** Member of the Council of Public Affairs of the Church. Initiated October 13th, 1966. Code name Mave.
- **Antonio Gregagnin.** He is the Tribune of First Causes for Beatification for Canonisation. Initiated October 19th, 1967. Code name Grea.
- **Giovanni Caprile.** Director of Catholic Civil Affairs. Initiated September 5th, 1957. Code name Gica.
- **Roberto Tucci.** Director-General of the Vatican Radio. A most important post since this station emits news round the clock in thirty-two languages. Initiated June 27th, 1957. Code name Turo.
- **Virgilio Levi.** Assistant-Director of the Vatican daily newspaper *L'Osservatore Romano,* and of Vatican Radio Station. Initiated July 4th, 1958. Code name Vile.

There are 526 Masonic Lodges in Italy. In view of that, their admitted membership of only 20,000 is questionable.

The French Register of Secret Societies is more closely guarded than the Italian, so that particulars of recent initiations cannot be quoted. The most sustained list of clerics belonging to French secret societies covers a few decades preceding the French Revolution, and it numbered, even at a time when infiltration of the Church by its enemies was on a smaller scale than it soon attained, some 256 members.

Part Six

When money speaks, the truth remains silent.

Russian proverb.

The adventurer Michele Sindona was already at the head of a vast financial empire when his friend Pope Paul VI, in 1969, made use of his services as financial adviser to the Vatican. The Sicilian's influence on both sides of the Atlantic was sufficient to ensure that he received universal respect; irrespective of personal character. The American ambassador in Rome referred to Sindona as 'the man of the year,' and *Time* magazine was later to call him 'the greatest Italian since Mussolini.'

His connection with the Vatican increased his status, and his business operations, carried out with the dexterity of a spider spinning a web, soon placed him on a near footing with the more political and publicly advertised Rothschilds and Rockefellers. He burrowed into banks and foreign exchange agencies, outwitted partners as well as rivals, and always emerged in a controlling capacity.

He invested money under assumed or other persons' names, disposing of and diverting funds, always with set purpose, and he pulled strings for the underground activities of the Central Intelligence Agency as well as for more secret bodies, that brought about political repercussions in European centres. All this was done with an air of confidential propriety and by methods that would not have survived the most casual examination, carried out by the most inefficient accountant.

One of his early banking contacts was with Hambro, and from that followed a list that came to include the Privata Italiana, Banca Unione, and the Banco di Messina, a Sicilian bank that he later owned. He held a majority stake in the Franklin National Bank of New York, controlled a network that covered nine banks, and became vice-president of three of them. The real assets of those banks were transferred to tax shelters such as Switzerland, Luxembourg, and Liberia.

Before long he had taken over the Franklin National, with its 104 branches and assets of more than five billion dollars, despite an American law that forbade direct ownership of any bank by groups with other financial interests. But a way round this was found by the then President Nixon, and by Sindona's friend and share manipulator David Kennedy, a former secretary to the United States treasury and that country's ambassador to Nato.

At one time it was reckoned that the amount involved in his foreign speculations alone exceeded twenty billion dollars. Apart from the interests already named, two Russian banks and the National Westminster were finger deep in his transactions. He was president of seven Italian companies, and the managing director of several more, with shares in the Paramount Pictures Corporation, Mediterranean Holidays, and the Dominican sugar trade. He had a voice on the board of Libby's, the Chicago food combine. He bought a steel foundry in Milan.

It was only to be expected that, when estimating such a man, his past and his character counted for less than the jingle in his pocket. New friends, acquaintances, public figures, and distant relatives pressed forward for a sight of the Sindona smile; and among them was a churchman, Monsignor Ameleto Tondini. Through him the financier met Messimo Spada, who managed the affairs of the Vatican bank, or, to give it a more innocuous title, the Institute for Religious Works.

Its main concern was with the handling of Vatican investments, which to some extent came under a body known as the Patrimony of the Apostolic See. That had come into existence, as a financial entity, in 1929, under one of the conditions of the Lateran Treaty concluded with Mussolini.

It had since outgrown the limitations imposed by the Treaty, and had taken on truly international dimensions under a conglomerate of bankers including John Pierpont Morgan of New York, the Paris Rothschilds, and the Hambros Bank of London. Its clerical supervisor was Monsignor (soon to be Cardinal) Sergio Guerri.

Spada, who was the chairman of Lancia, became chairman of a part ecclesiastical, part financial institution, known as the Pius XII Foundation for the Lay Apostleship, a very wealthy concern which was later taken over by Cardinal Villot, who was in many ways a reflection of Paul VI.

2.

There is always a sinister side to big money dealings, and one of Sindona's associates, Giorgio Ambrosoli, became increasingly nervous as the carrying out of increasing frauds kept pace with the profits, and with the effects they produced in several European social, economic, and political structures. He expressed his doubts to Sindona, who brushed them aside. But he did not do the same with Ambrosoli. Instead he made him the object of rumour and surrounded him with a network of suspicion. And one more unsolved crime was added to the Italian police register when Ambrosoli was shot dead outside his house by 'unknown assassins.'

Even before Sindona was concerned with its investment policy the Vatican, despite its condemnation of money-power in the past, was heavily involved in the capitalist system. It had interests in the Rothschild Bank in France, and in the Chase Manhattan Bank with its fifty-seven branches in forty-four countries; in the Credit Suisse in Zurich and also in London; in the Morgan Bank, and in the Banker Trust. It had large share holdings in General Motors, General Electric, Shell Oil, Gulf Oil, and in Bethlehem Steel.

Vatican representatives figured on the board of Finsider which, with its capital of 195 million lire spread through twenty-four companies, produced ninety per cent of Italian steel, besides controlling two shipping lines and the Alfa Romeo firm. Most of the Italian luxury hotels, including the Rome Hilton, were also among the items that figured in the Vatican share portfolio.

Sindona's influence at the Vatican, deriving from his earlier friendship with Paul VI, and the recent meetings with Spada, was soon felt in much the same way as it had been in the outer world. He assumed complete control of the Banca Privata. He bought the Feltrinelli publishing house, and the Vatican shared in its income despite the fact that some of its productions included calls to street violence and secret society propaganda. The same quarter gave support to Left-wing Trades Unions, and to the none too healthy work, often on the seamy side of the law, conducted by the Central Intelligence Agency. The same lack of discernment was shown by the fact that one of the firms that helped to swell the Sindona Vatican funds had been making, at least for a time, contraceptive pills.[14]

Other and more direct Vatican commitments were with the Ceramica Pozzi which supplied taps, sanitary equipment, and bidets, and with a chemical group, again with Hambros in the background, that manufactured synthetic fibres for textiles. Vatican representatives appeared on the boards of Italian and Swiss banks, and their influence was increasingly felt in the management of holding companies in many parts of the Western world.

Another 'shut eye' operation was when Cardinal Casaroli concluded an agreement with Communist authorities, whereby one of the Vatican companies erected a factory in Budapest.

Almost within hearing distance of the work was another Cardinal, Mindszenty, Archbishop of Hungary who, abandoned by Rome because of his anti-Communist stand, had taken refuge in the American Embassy after the abortive 1956 uprising.

Had it been possible to conduct a genuine inquiry at that time, the names of Vatican officials would have been found figuring in some of President Nixon's complicated ventures. So much emerges when, by steering a way through a mass of often contradictory manoeuvres, one pin-points the Vatican ownership of the General Immobiliare, one of the world's largest construction companies which dealt in land speculation, built motorways and the Pan Am offices, to quote but a few of its

---

[14] Yet Pope Paul criticised the capitalist system in his social encyclical Populorum Progressio on the development of peoples.

operations, and also controlled a major part of the Watergate complex in Washington.

It was thereby enabled to build, and own, the series of luxury buildings on the banks of the River Potomac that became the headquarters of the Democratic electoral campaign in 1972.

The management of the Generale Immobiliare was in the hands of Count Enrico Galeazzi, the director of an investment and credit company (estimated capital twenty-five billion lire), who could so freely come and go at the Vatican that he was known as the laypope.

The Holy See became a substantial partner in Sindona's commercial and industrial empire in the spring of 1969 when, in answer to calls from Paul VI, the financier made several visits to the Vatican where the two men met, in the Pope's study on the third floor, at midnight. (Only, so far as the minor clerics and staff of the Vatican were concerned, and according to the Pope's appointment book that was duly 'doctored' before being entered up, it was not His Holiness who conferred with Sindona but Cardinal Guerri, who in all probability was sleeping at the time.) Besides wishing to fortify the Vatican's investment policy, the Pope was concerned with maintaining the Church's non-liability for Government control, in the shape of tax, of its currency and assets. That exemption, with the Christian Democrats heading a four-party coalition since the end of the Second World War, had never been seriously questioned. But new voices were now being heard. The Vatican was named as the biggest tax-evader in postwar Italy, and there was a growing demand for its arrears to be settled.

Another member of this sanctified business circle was Paul Marcinkus, one of a Lithuanian family who had emigrated to Chicago. He was in the good books of Monsignor Pasquali Macchi, the Pope's personal secretary, and had so far not been prominent in any pastoral field. His most practical experience, in the sphere of Church activity had been gained when, due to his standing six feet four in his socks, and his long powerful arms (which earned him the nickname of 'gorilla') he supervised the guarding of Paul VI during his travels. Paul made him a Bishop.

As controller of the Vatican Bank, a post that was handed to him by Paul VI, he was responsible for more than 10,000 accounts belonging to Religious Orders and to private individuals, including the Pope. The number of the latter's account, by the way, was 16.16. He handled the Vatican's secret funds and its gold reserves at Fort Knox, and he transferred a substantial part of the funds, in the hope of making a quick profit, to the Sindona holdings.

He was also President of the Institute for Religious Training, and a director of the Continental Illinois Bank of Nassau. His rise was neither unexpected nor brought about without influence being exerted, for on July 2nd, 1963, Marcinkus followed the example of those many clerics who, in defiance of Canon 2335, had joined a secret society. His code name was Marpa.

Taking advantage of the fact that clerical garb was no longer essential, Marcinkus shouldered his way through the fringes, then into the colourful noisy heart, of Roman society. He was the affluent manager of one of the city's most influential, privileged, and respected banks. He lounged at bars, joined exclusive clubs that had hitherto been envied and far-off places to him, and showed his animal strength on the links by sending numerous golf balls into oblivion. In time his blatant playboy attitude annoyed the more established Roman community, who turned a cold shoulder. It would seem that he had little more than gangling brawn to recommend him. But there were always plenty of Americans, who were there on business, to take their place, though even they were shocked when the Bishop was said to be involved in fraudulent bankruptcy.

Meanwhile the first warnings, conveyed by hints of danger, were reaching Sindona and the Vatican from many parts of the world. The current call was to transfer money to the United States, as events in Europe pointed to political unrest and economic collapse; and the future of the Franklin Bank, in which Sindona and the Vatican were heavily involved, became highly doubtful following a series of disastrous speculations. There were frantic efforts to persuade more secure banks to buy outright, or at least re-float, the Franklin. Calls went out from Montini to arrange the transfer of Vatican investments to a safer haven.

It was not that Sindona had lost his touch; but world forces, assisted by enemies in the Mafia who envied Sindona's rise, were proving too much for the maintenance of far-flung ventures like some over which he had presided. Aware that he was standing on shaky ground, Sindona tried to gain the support of the Nixon administration, by offering a million dollars, which perhaps could have materialised only if the deal had been accepted, for the President's electoral fund. But as Sindona, for obvious reasons, insisted on not being named, and since the acceptance of anonymous gifts for an election was forbidden by law, his offer was declined. It was disappointing for all concerned that it impinged upon one of the few laws that even the elastic Federal system could not openly stretch.

Sindona made a final gesture in the approved style of a Hollywood gangster. He threw a lavish and spectacular evening party at Rome's foremost hotel (that was probably owned by the Vatican) which was attended by the American ambassador; Cardinal Caprio (who had been in charge of Vatican investments before the arrival of Marcinkus), and the accommodating Cardinal Guerri.

Marcinkus merely came in for a great deal of blame. His operations with Vatican funds, said Monsignor Benelli, one of his critics, had been intolerable. But Marcinkus, who knew too much of what went on behind the scenes at the Vatican, could not be abandoned, and he was given a diplomatic post in the Church.

Sindona had been tipped off, by one of his hirelings who was also employed by the secret service, that a warrant was out for his arrest. But he bluffed and drank his way through the festivities, went off for a time to his luxury villa in Geneva, then took a plane to New York.

There, pending actual charges, he was kept under a form of mild surveillance.

But it seems that some of those who were detailed to watch him belonged to the Mafia, and the next the Pope heard of his former adviser was that he had been shot and wounded in a scuffle.

It was easy enough, by delving into his past that was more than ankle-deep in great and petty swindles, and now that he was no longer a power to be reckoned with, to bring him to trial; and an attempted kidnap case, and widespread bribery, were now added to the charges against him. When the obliging Cardinal Guerri heard of this, he seems to have become suddenly convinced, perhaps because his name had figured in talks that clinched the bargaining between Pontiff and financier, that Sindona was a much maligned man. He wanted to go to New York and testify on his behalf.

But the Pope, aware of Guerri's easy-going nature, and not wanting the extent of his own co-operation with the accused to be dragged out in the witness box, kept Guerri in Rome.

The trial ended, in the autumn of 1980, with Sindona receiving a sentence of twenty-five years' imprisonment. Few, apart from those members of the public who expressed indignation as the financial antics of Sindona were made known to them for the first time, believe that such a sentence will ever be served. At least one anti-clerical paper suggested that Pope Paul was lucky not to have been put on the stand alongside his banker.

As it was, the Pope was left with two reminders of their partnership. The Church had sustained a heavy financial loss which meant, as the Pope asserted with a quite gratuitous beating of the breast, that the Bride of Christ was face to face with bankruptcy; while there was a new administrative agency for finance that he had founded as a result of Sindona's help.

At the head of this was Cardinal Vagnozzi, Apostolic Delegate in New York. He was assisted by Cardinal Hoeffner, of Cologne, and Cardinal John Cody of Chicago.

3.

The last named of that trio was soon to make a sensational entry into the news. Cardinal John Patrick Cody, aged seventy-three, the son of a St. Louis fireman, was Archbishop of the largest Roman Catholic diocese in America. He therefore had the handling of many thousands of tax-exempt ecclesiastical funds. And in the autumn of 1981 his congregation was overwhelmed, as only loyal Church members can be, by rumours that soon became facts, to the effect that the United States Attorney's office in Chicago was looking into Cody's financial affairs.

A Federal Grand Jury had also asked for the records of a St. Louis investment company, where a certain Mrs. Helen Dolan Wilson had an account; to be examined.

The inquiry, most unusual in the case of a contemporary Cardinal, turned upon what was called the diverting, disposition, or misuse of Church funds amounting to more than £500,000 in English money. It also came to light that the National Conference of Catholic Bishops had lost more than four million dollars in a single year, during which time the Cardinal had been treasurer.

The Mrs. Wilson referred to, of the same age as the Cardinal, was variously referred to as a relation of his by marriage, as his sister, as a niece, while Cody usually spoke of her as his cousin.

Her father, more precise judgments claimed, had married the Cardinal's aunt, while others were sure that no real blood relationship existed between them. The couple concerned said that a brother and sister relationship, begun in their childhood in St. Louis, was their only tie.

'We were raised together,' explained Mrs. Wilson. Their remaining close friends was therefore a natural development. They travelled together, and for the past twenty-five years she had followed his every move about the diocese. He had become, in the religious sense, her 'supervisor,' a role that she found beneficial when her marriage, which left her with a son, ended in the divorce court.

It was easy enough for the Cardinal to place her, as manager, in an office connected with the Church in St. Louis. Her appearances there were far from regular but, whether working or not, she nonetheless remained on the Church's pay-roll. He also helped her son to set up business, in the same town, as an insurance agent, a post that Wilson resigned when, with the Cardinal, he started dealing in 'real estate.'

Mrs. Wilson retired, after having earned a modest £4,000 a year, but before long she was known to be worth nearly a million dollars, mostly in stocks and bonds. She was also the beneficiary of a hundred thousand dollars insurance policy, taken out on the Cardinal's life, on which she borrowed.

The inquiries made by the Federal Grand Jury, and publicised by the Chicago *Tribune* and *Sun-Times*, brought forth a flood of allegations. The Cardinal had made over most of the missing money to her. Part of it had gone in buying her a house at Boca Raton, in Florida: There had also been a luxury car, expensive clothes and furs, and holiday cash presents.

The Cardinal, though saddened and feeling rejected because of the allegations, was firm in saying that he didn't need a chance to contradict them. He was ready to forgive all those responsible. Mrs. Wilson was equally firm in saying that she had received no money from the Cardinal. To say that there was anything more than friendship between them was a vicious lie, or even a joke. She strongly resented being scandalised, and being portrayed as a kept woman or (as her fellow-countrymen put it) à tramp.'

Had it not been for the many falls from grace that have overtaken the modern Church, a case like this would scarcely have merited more than a mention. But now it prompts questions. Was it a frame-up, part of the age-long wish to bring the Church into disrepute? Was the Cardinal personally corrupt? Or was he one of the infiltrators who, without any real religious conviction, have been secretly fostered into the Church for the sole purpose of wearing away its moral and traditional fabric?

There is, in the light of other strange happenings that have occurred, nothing extravagant in that suggestion; and it would seem to be borne out by a long report in *The Chicago Catholic* of September 29th, 1978. An Archdiocesan Liturgical Congress was held in order, as one of the jargon-crazed Modernists said, to keep the Church 'living, moving, changing, growing, becoming new, after some centuries of partial paralysis.'

As part of that process, dance groups frolicked under flashing multi-coloured lights, trumpets blared, people reached and scrambled for gas-filled balloons, and donned buttons that bore the message Jesus loves us;' while a priest, who was looked upon as an expert in the new liturgy, his face whitened like a clown's, paraded about in a top hat and with a grossly exaggerated potbelly emerging from the cloak he wore.

The background to all this was made up of vestments, banners, and the hotch-potch of a mural, all of which, in the approved style of 'modern art,' revealed no more than casually applied splashes of paint. The Mass that marked the close of this truly ridiculous Congress (that, as we shall see, was only a faint reflection of what happened elsewhere, and which would never have been dreamt of before the days of 'Good Pope John') was presided over by Cardinal Cody.

At another time *The Chicago Tribune,* in a report describing what was said to be a Gays' altar,' referred to a concelebration (meaning celebration of the Eucharist by two or more priests) at a church in that city: One hundred and twenty-two priests were present at what passed for Mass, and every one of them was a self-confessed moral pervert.

Neither of these profanities called forth a word of protest from John Patrick, Cardinal Cody.

He died of a heart attack in April, 1982, while this book was in preparation.

Part Seven

Woe to him who doesn't know how to wear his mask, be he King or Pope.

Pirandello.

The give-and-take of human relationships poses a more difficult problem than those that are normally accredited to science. For the latter will, in all probability, be solved in time; but when it comes to people, especially those who are no longer among the living, we are faced with questions that, in this our world, are unlikely to be answered.

For instance, it has to be asked why did two prelates, within a few months of each other, both die in circumstances that are not normally connected with any churchman, and, more especially in these cases, highly placed ones?

When a party of Parisians, after having attended a religious festival in the country, returned to the capital late at night on Sunday, May 19th, 1974, some of them noticed that the priest who had been in charge of them looked ill and tired.

He was Jean Danielou, sixty-nine years old, and a Cardinal; no cut and dried character, but someone difficult to place in the minds of ordinary people who knew very little about him. He had entered a Jesuit novitiate in 1929, and had been ordained nine years later. The author of fourteen books on theology, and the Head of the Theological Faculty at the University of Paris, he was also a member of the Academie Française.

While revealing little, he made certain statements about himself that invited questions; even controversy. 'I am naturally a pagan, and a Christian only with difficulty,' was one of them, though that, of course, expresses a point a view held by many of his creed who know that little more than a knife edge exists between affirmation and disbelief. He was aware of new elements, that were forming and gathering strength within the Church, and although he judged freely-A kind of fear has spread leading to real intellectual capitulation in the face of carnal excesses-' the conservatives were no more able to number him among their kind than were the more vocal progressives. He was one of the founders, in 1967, of the Fraternity of Abraham, an interfaith group comprising the three monotheistic religions, Islam, Judaism, and Christianity.

'Today is a time when we sin against intelligence.' Both sides could have claimed that as a dictum. Some accused him, when he appeared to hold back, of being prudish. But always he claimed to be uncommitted. Ì feel in the depths of my being that I am a free man.' But freedom, when it is not a political catch-word, can no more be tolerated in the world than truth (as the peasant girl Joan of Arc had realised centuries before). And the more Danielou withdrew from society, and lived quietly at his residence in the Rue Notre-Dame des Champs, without keeping a secretary or running a car, the more he became suspect, or openly disliked.

None of this escaped him, but he tried not to dwell upon it. Had he done so, he owned that he would have been discouraged, a self-evident failure who had not taken advantage of the promise that was made available by his rise in the Church. Later he found, or at least came to believe, that opponents were scheming and plotting against him. There was, indeed, a definite campaign of whispers and hints in the Press that compelled him, though it was more a matter of choice than the force of actual opposition, to maintain a steadily but relatively unimpressive place on the fringe of things.

So he remained, a problematic figure who arrived home on that Sunday midnight after an exhausting day in the country. But

Monday brought no change in his routine. He said Mass, as usual, at eight o'clock, then worked in his office and received a few visitors. He lunched at a restaurant, and afterwards called at the home of a Professor at the Sorbonne.

It appears, for some unexplained reason, that part of his mail went to an address in the Rue Monsieur; for he collected this, was back at his house at three o'clock, then left a quarter of an hour later, after saying that he expected to return at five.

But he did not. For at three forty-eight the police received an urgent message from a Madame Santoni, who occupied an upper floor at number fifty-six in the Rue Dulong, a none too reputable quarter just north of the Boulevard des Batignolles. Her message brought the police rushing to the scene, for it told them that no less a person than a Cardinal was dead on her premises.

He, Danielou, had called there soon after three-thirty. He had, so someone told her, run up the stairs four at a time, then collapsed at the top, purple in the face, and soon became unconscious. She had torn his clothes apart, and summoned help. But it was impossible to revive him, and the first arrivals had been helplessly looking on when his heart stopped.

In answer to a radio announcement of the Cardinal's death, the Apostolic Nuncio, with the Jesuit Provincial of France, and Father Coste, Superior of the Jesuits in Paris, arrived at the apartment, together with reporters from the *France Soir,* and nuns who were called in to deal with the body that was, however, already too rigid to be prepared for the funeral.

Father Coste addressed the reporters. It was essential for them to maintain the utmost discretion, and having said that he went on to state that the Cardinal had died in the street, or it may possibly have been on the stairway, after he had fallen in the street.

Oh no, it wasn't,' broke in Madame Santoni. Father Coste objected to her interruption, the other clerics joined in, the police had their say, the reporters asked questions, and at the height of the argument, although no one actually witnessed her going, Madame Santoni disappeared and was seen no more at the inquiry.

Now the lady in question thoroughly deserved the title of Madame. She was well known to the police and to the Press, a twenty-four year old blonde who traded under the name of Mimi, sometimes as hostess at a bar, a go-go girl at an all night cabaret, or as a strip-tease dancer in the Pigalle. She was never on call at her home, which was run as a bawdy-house by her husband. It was then, however, temporarily out of business, as he had been convicted only three days previously for pimping.

Such explanations as the Church chose to offer were vague, and all in line with the general verdict that the Cardinal had burst a blood-vessel, or suffered a heart attack. Cardinal Marty, the Archbishop of Paris, refused a request from Catholics as well as from secular quarters for an inquiry to be held into the Cardinal's death. After all, he explained, the Cardinal wasn't there to speak for himself. It may have been an unfortunate afterthought that caused the Archbishop to speak of the Cardinal needing to defend himself. The eulogy was delivered in Rome by Cardinal Garrone who said: 'God grant us pardon. Our existence cannot fail to include an element of weakness and shadow.'

One may wonder how deep Garrone's soul-searching may have gone since, although he was known to belong to a secret society, he brazenly sat it out and held on to his red hat. A comment by the orthodox journal *La* Croix was briefer and more to the point:

'Whatever the truth is, we Christians well know that each of us is a sinner.'

This sort of happening supplied the Left-wing anti-clerical papers with copy for a week. One such, *Le Canard Enchaîné*,[15] had scored heavily some years before, in a controversy over the ownership of a string of brothels within a few yards of the cathedral in Le Mans. The paper claimed that they were owned by a high dignitary of the Church. His friends and colleagues strongly denied this. But the paper was proved to have been right.

---

[15] This is a slightly more radical French equivalent of Private *Eye*.

Now the same source had no hesitation in saying that the Cardinal had been leading a double life.

He had been under observation for some time, a step that was ordered by no less a person than M. Chirac, the Prime Minister. He and Jacques Foccard, a former Minister of the Interior, both knew perfectly well that the Cardinal had been paying regular visits to Mimi.

That in turn was ridiculed by Danielou's supporters; whereupon the paper retorted that there might be more revelations to come. If we were to publish all the details, it would be enough to shut you up for the rest of your natural days.'

The truth of this strange story may lie in one of four possible explanations.

One may have its origin in the effects of the Second Vatican Council. Danielou was said by some to have regarded that as a positive disaster, and we know that he described the more liberal school of theologians, to which the Council gave rise, as lamentable, miserable, execrable, wretched. Many resented this, especially when he went on to call them assassins of the Faith.' He determined to do what he could to prevent the Faith being secularised and degraded, and this led him to think, since human tempers are just as hot within the Church as they are outside it, that he was in danger. That would account for the somewhat enclosed life he led in Paris.

But he let it be known that he was determined to make a stand, and he drew up a list of those he called traitors to the Church. Some of those whose names were included breathed fire against him, but he publicly announced that he intended to publish the list.

Four days later, according to a theory held by many who are certainly not light-weights, he was murdered by those he would have named. Then, inspired by a kind of macabre humour, those he had called 'assassins' had his body taken out and dumped in a brothel. After that, the surprising discovery could easily be arranged.

That is written in full knowledge of how outrageous it must appear to those who regard the Church from a purely parochial level; in happy ignorance of its medieval history that was destined to be repeated, with all the cut-and-thrust and poisoned cups of that period, in a few years' time, and within the very walls of the Vatican palace.

Or could Danielou have been, earlier in life, one of those infiltrators whose influence he came to detest? Did he, after being initiated into one of the secret societies opposed to the Church, undergo a change of heart, which caused him to be looked upon as a menace? There is ample evidence that the societies had, and still have, no scruples in dealing with defaulters.

That suggestion is not without substance. For in the Rue Puteaux, Paris, there is an ancient church, the crypt of which serves as the Grand Temple of the Grand Lodge of France. Some three years before Danielou's death the Auxiliary Bishop of Paris, Daniel Pezeril, had there been received into the Lodge, after he had issued a communique to justify his action. In it he said: 'It is not the Church which has changed. On the contrary, Masonry has evolved.' It was Monsignor Pezeril who was asked, by Pope Paul, to seek a way of bridging the gap between the Church and the societies.

Cardinal Danielou had been a not infrequent visitor to the crypt, where he was seen in consultation with one of the Lodge Masters who had been honoured with the title of Grand Secretary of the Obedience. It must therefore be asked, does the answer to the mystery lie with those with whom Danielou had conferred in the crypt?

But the story circulated by the satirical papers was the most shrill and insistent, and the most commonly known. They claimed that it had been obvious, to those who had been in Madame Mimi's apartment before the police arrived, that Danielou's body had been hurriedly dressed. And if he had not been one of her clients, why had he gone there with three thousand francs that were found in his pocket-book?

The purveyors of such scandal concluded that the Cardinal had died in a state of ecstasy, if not of grace.

Yet another version brings the story more up to date, with a trial that has now (the time is November, 1981) passed through its opening stage in Paris.

On Christmas Eve, 1976, Prince Jean de Broglie was shot dead by a gunman as he left a friend's house. The necessary inquiries brought a far reaching web of fraud, complicity, and blackmail into the open, involving the former President Giscard d'Estaing and a friend of his, Prince Michel Poniatowski.

The latter had recently ousted and taken the place of Jacques Foccard as Minister of the Interior, and Foccard was now using a woman, who was known also to Giscard, to get money from the Prince. Foccard has already been mentioned in connection with the Danielou case.

Since the known operation is obviously part of a vast cover-up it is no more possible, than it is necessary here, to unravel the details, which leave all those concerned in a very murky light. But it is claimed that they account for Danielou's being in the brothel, and for the three thousand francs that were found on his person. They were one of the instalments that he had been paying, for the past three months, on behalf of someone, referred to as a friend of his, who was being blackmailed.

A most disarming finale to all this came in the form of a line or two in an English religious weekly, the *Catholic Herald*, which briefly announced that Cardinal Danielou had died in Paris.

2.

Brief though the memory of the public is, there may have been a few lingering thoughts on Cardinal Danielou's mysterious death in the minds of some Parisians who noticed a Bishop from the south-west of their country step from a train on the afternoon of January the 12th, 1975.

He was Monsignor Roger Tort, fifty-seven years old, and Bishop of Montauban, on the River Tam just north of Toulouse. He was due to attend a meeting of the French Episcopal Commission, and he straightway proceeded to a room he had booked at the headquarters of the Catholic Aid Society in the Rue de Bac. His movements for the next couple of days are unrecorded, but on Thursday the 15th he lunched at the Commission's meeting place in the Rue du Regard, on the left bank of the Seine. It is possible that from there he went to meet a friend whom he had known during the war, but we know nothing certain about him until an alarm was raised, and a call went out to the police, on the night of the 16th.

Excitement centred on the Rue du Ponceau, again on the left bank, a narrow street off the Rue Saint-Denis, a quarter notorious for brothels, prostitutes, and sex shops, where red lamps shone invitingly. The woman who raised the alarm kept one of the brothels. She had come across a man, who was obviously ill, in the street outside her door, and she got the help of two others of her kind to drag him inside. By then he was dead.

Who was he? She neither knew nor cared. She had never seen him before. She had done what she could from purely 'humanitarian reasons.' The red lamps winked as more people arrived and the contradictory stories went on. The stranger had died of a heart attack, between seven and eleven o'clock, in the street, or in the corridor, or in one of the rooms. A news-hungry reporter said that the Bishop, once his identity had been confirmed, had come a long way from his lodgings and from the Commission's meeting place. The reporter went on to say, backed by a snap judgment from the police that, as in the case of Danielou, the body appeared to have been hastily dressed.

A clerical apologist later advised all those interested to put away such thoughts as being totally unworthy. He pointed out- that Monsignor Tort, when found, was still wearing his Bishop's ring, and his pectoral cross, and that his rosary was still in his pocket. Surely the presence of those objects was enough to prove that 'no inadmissible intentions' had brought him into the district?

The facts, so far as they could be known, did not admit of any shameful interpretation.

The Church absolved the dead man from moral guilt, and within a few weeks a new Bishop was being installed at the small cathedral in Montauban.

An elementary reading of these two episodes could be taken as evidence that churchmen (especially Catholic ones and, more especially, those of exalted status) may be hypocritical and corrupt. That, of course, will not be disputed by any save the wilfully blind; and the fact that they may be members of secret societies, first and last, and therefore void of genuine religious conviction, is the theme of these pages. But there is no evidence to connect the deaths.

In the Cardinal's case there are signs, however tentative, that he had been persuaded to act a minor role in a major political scandal; or that he had taken a definite stand in a religious quarrel; and religious quarrels, like a civil war, admit of no quarter being given. There is, however, no trace of Monsignor Tort being involved in anything startling. He can only be the object of assumption-that he was the victim of personal weakness, of an accident, or of someone's wish to discredit religion.

But as it is, the similarity between the two deaths is startling.

Part Eight

> *Christian atmosphere, Christian tradition and morality ... is diminishing and is in fact to a great extent displaced by a way of life and thought opposed to the Christian one.*
>
> Pope Pius XII.

This section is concerned with some of the most dramatic changes in the whole of history; changes whose ultimate significance has, in the popular sense, gone largely unreported, and because of that they have been accepted without comment by the world at large. But they are changes that have set the tone of our present; they are fashioning our future; and in time to come they will be so established that it will seem foolish, or eccentric, to question them. At the risk of being tedious, and in order to emphasise a vital point, it needs to be repeated that religious Rome was regarded, less than a generation ago, as the one fixed centre of faith that would not change. It was proof against novelty. It despised fashion and towered above what is called the spirit of the age.

Secure in itself, it admitted no speculation, none of the guesswork that too often goes by the name of discovery. It maintained one attitude and taught, century after century, one message that was always the same. So much was claimed by itself, endorsed by its followers, and recognised by its enemies.

But just as in our time we have witnessed the spread of Communism, so at the turn of the century another movement threatened what may be called the more static ordering of thought. It was, put very roughly, a mingling of the nineteenth century's liberal and scientific preoccupations, and its object was to treat the Bible to the same sort of criticism to which the political and scientific worlds had been subjected. Evolution, as opposed to settled and accepted truth, was in the air; dogma was questioned, and many saw this, though some of its propagators may not have intended it to go so far, as a denial of supernatural religion.

The reigning Pope of the time, Pius X, denounced Modernism, as the new movement was called, as being no less than freethought, a most dangerous heresy. An encyclical, issued in 1907, and a condition he laid down a few years later, that clergy were required to take an anti-Modernist oath, evidenced his firm opposition. And a similar situation was created later when Pius XII, brought face to face with Communism, condemned it time and again, and in 1949 promulgated the sentence of excommunication against any Catholic who countenanced or supported it in any way.

But a very considerable difference soon appeared between the receptions that greeted the opposition expressed by the two Popes. Pius X had been accused, in the main, of arrogance and intolerance. But Pius XII, echoing the sentiments of Pius IX, Leo XIII, and Pius XI, was not only ridiculed by avant-garde journalists, one of whom called him a small-town aristocrat,' but was actually opposed and contradicted by the man who in 1963 ascended the Papal throne as Paul VI.

His sympathy for Left-wing politics had never been in doubt. He had co-operated with Communists. His encyclical Populorum Progressio, issued in 1967 on the development of the world, was adversely criticised by the Wall Street Journal as 'warmed up Marxism.'[16] But his being ranged openly on their side, and his reversal of earlier Papal judgments, marked a new departure in a

---

[16] Robert Kaiser, who approved the innovations of Vatican Two.

Pontiff whose words carried to the greater part of the Christian world.

He was fully in tune with the modern age, and responsive to the currents of the time. He was ready to open doors that every one of his predecessors, even those of doubtful character, had kept fastened. This was made clear in 1969, when he said: 'We are about to witness a greater freedom in the life of the Church, and therefore in that of her children. This freedom will mean fewer obligations, and fewer inward prohibitions. Formal disciplines will be reduced ... every form of intolerance and absolutism will be abolished.'

Such statements were welcomed by some, while others among his listeners were filled with apprehension; and when he referred to some normally accepted religious standpoints as being warped, and entertained only by those who were polarised or extremist, the hopes or fears of both modes of thought appeared to be justified. Was he paving the way for what would virtually be a new religion, freed from established notions and practices, and embracing all the advantages of the modern world, or was he bent on so paring down the established religion until, instead of standing out as decisive, unique, it appeared to be but one faith among many?

So the two sides waited. One in favour of a promised relaxation, the other apprehensive lest many of their traditional supports were about to be dismantled.

2.

Here again, I feel it necessary to repeat, what follows is neither in the nature of attack nor of defence. It is a simple summary of events that occurred, and of declarations made; and if they appear to be partisan it is not the fault of the present writer, but of Pope Paul who made them all of one character.

He challenged and condemned the unbroken front presented by Pius X in the face of Modernism. The latter's imposition of an anti-Modernist oath was said to have been an error, so Paul abolished it. The Index of forbidden books, and the prerogatives of the Holy Office with its historic right to impose interdicts and excommunication, were now things of the past. The Canon Laws of the Church, hitherto regarded as pillars, the guardians and promulgators of decisions and judgments, were thrown open to criticism and, if need be, to revision. History and text-books, written from a predominantly Catholic viewpoint, were blue-pencilled or re-edited.

The Church's contacts with the world, and with other religions, were to be more open, and no longer conducted from a height of superior authority, knowledge, and experience. There was declared to be no fixation of absolute truth. Discussion or dialogue was to take the place of declaration. And from these changes a new society of humanist culture would emerge, with an ostensible Catholic background provided by advanced theologians who, under Pius XII, had been kept on the fringes of the Church.

They included Hans Kung, whose views were said to be more anti-orthodox than those advanced by Luther. He was to claim that he had been specially defended by Paul VI. The German Jesuit, Karl Rahner, whose brand of thought had formerly been frowned upon as being too extreme, was now told by Paul to forge ahead.' The Dominican Schillebeeckx spread consternation among the already dispirited Dutch clergy with such statements as that Christianity would, sooner or later, have to surrender to atheism, as the most honest and natural man was the one who believed nothing.

Teachers such as these, far from being reprimanded, retained their secure positions and were given a publicity, not usually accorded to churchmen, in the Press. Even an Irish paper referred to Hans Kung and to Schillebeeckx as 'the most outstanding theologians in the world:' and the belief that they were confident of having powerful support was strengthened when it became known, in some ecclesiastical quarters, that prelates such as Suenens and Alfrink had threatened to form a 'Cardinals' Trade Union' if Hans Kung and his writings were condemned.

The total ban on Communism and its supporters, by Pius XII, was taken for granted, although it had never been actually enforced. But even so there were demands for its removal.

Instead of an ice-bound resistance to Communism, that had been an accepted feature of the historic Church, a thaw set in, and it soon became no longer remarkable for a priest to speak and act in favour of Marxism. Some accompanied their change of heart with a profession of contempt for the past, as did Robert Adolphs, Prior of the influential Augustinian house of Eindhoven, in Holland.

Writing in *The Church is Different* (Burns and Oates), he said that the philosophy of St. Thomas Aquinas represented à pretty desiccated kind of Western thinking.' He denounced the antiModernism of Pius X as a 'Fascist-like movement within the Church,' and he ridiculed the

warnings given by Pius XII who had imagined that 'he had to do battle with a sort of underground Modernist conspiracy that was making use of a widespread clandestine organisation in order to undermine the foundation of the Catholic Church.'

The Flemish professor, Albert Dondeyne, was more outspoken in *Geloof en Wereld, (Belief and the World)*, where he criticised the mental outlook of the Church for always having been convinced as to the total perfidy of Communism. He referred to the Church's habit of presenting things as though Christianity were simply and without reminder opposed to the Communistic order of society as being extremely dangerous.

'Christian society,' he went on, 'makes God the servant of a kind of Christian party interest.

It may,' he continued, identify Communism with the Devil; but what if this particular Devil has been conjured up by the errors and shortcomings of Christianity itself?' He admitted that the inhuman aspect of Marxism could not be denied. 'But this does not altogether preclude there being major positive values in Communism to which Christianity of the nineteenth century ought to have been open, and to which Christianity must all the while remain receptive today.'

A similar plea emanated from a most unexpected quarter, the semi-official Vatican newspaper *L'Osservatore Romano*, which recommended Catholics being taught to collaborate with Marxists for the common good. Communism, it was urged, had changed dramatically since the time of Lenin and of Stalin; and there was now no reason why the Church, if only because of its humanitarian aspect, should not regard it as an ally. Old differences between them were disappearing, and the Church should now recognise, as more than one Western European government was on the point of doing, that Communism had a vital part to play in helping to shape the future.

Traditionalists eyed these advances with no little alarm. As they saw it, a door was being opened by which Marxist elements could enter into their stronghold; and those fears increased when Communist and Vatican officials showed signs of entering into a partnership that had hitherto been unthinkable.

Prelates whose names might be known to the public, the ever serviceable Suenens, Willebrands, Bea, and Konig of Vienna, exhibited a readiness to walk hand-in-hand with agents hot from Moscow, who, but a short time before, had ridiculed the Church's claim to moral sovereignty over the minds of men. Nothing now was said of that claim by either side. Instead a list of everyday details, which maintained a steady growth over the years, showed how atheistic and orthodox spokesmen were passing from dialogue into a series of friendly exchanges.

Archbishop Casaroli, acting as middleman between the Vatican and the satellite States, flew in a Red airliner to the Soviet capital. He and members of the Central Committee raised glasses together in the Kremlin. He dined with K.G.B. officers in Bulgaria, and later in Czechoslovakia.

The secular Press circulated such items as proof that the Church had at last come down from its pedestal, and was accepting democracy; and the nervousness previously felt by traditionalists became downright fear when Paul VI, between the years *1967* and *1978*, by his own words and actions, gave evidence of that very definite shift in Vatican *policy*.

Let us telescope and summarise the allusive events of that time. Local armed risings in Africa were everywhere on the increase, and the Pope supported those movements even when they not infrequently led to the massacre of women and children. By a surprising turn-about he said that the Christians in those parts were the terrorists, and the whites the latter had displaced had always exerted an influence that was bad. When the Reds finally took over the provinces of Mozambique and Angola he hailed them as legitimate representatives of the people, and expressed a personal desire to meet some of the guerrilla leaders.

Three of them, Amilcar Cabral, Agostino Neto, and Marcellino dos Santos, accordingly went to the Vatican, where there was a kissing of hands as the Pope gave them a letter expressing *de* facto recognition of their Communist regime. But he was less forthcoming when a deputation showed him pictures, some revolting, of murderous activities carried out by West African terrorists.

Sceptical journalists exchanged knowing looks when he made very obvious efforts to put them aside.

Equally surprising was the affectionate respect he confessed for Obote of Uganda, who had a long record of violence behind him and who is, at the moment of writing, still in the news as being a more bloodthirsty tyrant than the overthrown Amin. The blacks of Uganda were actually urged by the Pope-it must be the first call of its kind ever to issue from such a quarter-to take up arms against the whites.

In Algiers, many of the half-million Catholics there, under Monsignor Duval, were slaughtered when the overwhelming Moslem population turned against them. Duval abandoned his charges and joined their enemies, an act of betrayal that was rewarded by Pope Paul creating him a Prince of the Church.

Another puzzling situation occurred in Spain, at a time when the shooting of police, by Basque gunmen, was at a startlingly high level. Five of the gunmen were caught and sentenced to death.

It was a time of grief for Pope Paul, who called the executions that followed à homicidal act of repression.' He offered special prayers, but only for the murderers.

Their victims were never mentioned. Thus encouraged by Rome, there was an upsurge of Communism in Mexico and in Latin-American States. Monsignor Ignaccio de Leon, speaking for the Mexican bishops, declared that his Church had shown itself to be useless in the face of social problems. Most fair-minded people will agree that it probably had. But no better example had been shown by the Marxism he openly preached from the pulpit.

Cardinal Henriquez celebrated a *Te Deum* in his cathedral when Salvador Allende, who boasted of being atheist, became President of Chile. Many Catholics, swayed by the hierarchy, had used their votes to help him to power. The name of Christ was now rarely heard in those once highly orthodox countries, except when it was used to invite a depreciatory comparison with such luminaries as Lenin and Mao Tse Tung. The revolutionary Fidel Castro of Cuba was honoured as a man inspired by God.'

Causes that excite suspicion are sometimes covered by euphemistic terms, and observers who were alarmed by Pope Paul's political leanings were liable to be assured that he was following à policy of expansionism:' But whatever their nature, his sympathies certainly extended over a wide area. He confessed to feeling close spiritual ties with Red China. He sent his accredited diplomatic agent to the Communist government in Hanoi. He voiced support for the atheistic regimes in Yugoslavia and Cuba. He entered into talks with the Russian controlled government of Hungary.

But he was less cordial in his relations with a traditionally orthodox country such as Portugal.

His presence there in May, *1967*, excited comment, both on account of the almost casual arrangements he made for meeting the Catholic President, Salazar, and the way in which (as one of his closest colleagues remarked) he practically mumbled when celebrating the Mass that marked the climax of his visit.

It had been taken for granted that he would welcome a meeting with Lucia dos Santos, the last survivor of the three children who, in *1917*, witnessed the apparitions, the strange phenomena that accompanied them, at the small town of Fatima. But the Pope put her aside with a testy:

'Now now, later.' As an afterthought he referred her to a bishop.

A different kind of reception was accorded to Claudia Cardinale and Gina Lollobrigida, when the Pope received them at the Vatican. They were certainly not dressed in the approved way for a Papal audience; and the crowd who had assembled to gape at the stars' expressed admiration for the Holy Father's broadmindedness.

This would seem to be the place to introduce a report that reached me by way of a, M. Maurice Guignard, a former student of the Society of Jesus at the college of St. Francis de Sales, Evreux, Normandy. The report, dated the 7th of August, 1972, originated from a body for the defence of the Faith, of Waterloo Place, Hanover. It was drawn up out of obedience' to orders given by Father Arrupe, Superior-General of the Society, and it was the work of Father Saenz Arriaga, Doctor of Philosophy and of Canon Law.

Apart from those influential Jesuits, it was substantiated and countersigned by the following members of the Society:

> - Cardinal Danielou, the story of whose mysterious death, in 1974, is told in part seven of this book.
> - Father Grignottes, private. secretary and confessor to Father Arrupe.
> - Father de Bechillon, former Rector of Evreux.
> - Father de Lestapis, formerly of Evreux and for some time in charge of Radio Vatican broadcasts.
> - Father Bosc, formerly professor at Evreux and Professor of Sociology at the University of Mexico.
> - Father Galloy, member of the faculty of the College of Lyons.

Dealing with the past of Paul VI, it states that from 1936 to 1950 he was prominent in a vast network of espionage that covered some of the countries, on both sides, involved in the Second World War.

It goes on to say that he was a principal shareholder, with a Maronite Archbishop,[17] of a chain of brothels in Rome. He found the money for various films, such as the erotic *Temptations of Marianne*, which he financed on condition that the leading role was given to a certain actress named Patricia Novarini. When not working at the movie studio, this young lady performed as a striptease artist at the Crazy Horse Saloon, an exclusive night-club in Rome.

The tolerance accorded to film stars was, however, withheld from those who refused, even at great cost to themselves, to compromise with the Russians. One such was Cardinal Slipyi who, as Patriarch of the Ukrainian Church, had witnessed the deaths, deportation, or the unexplained disappearance of some ten million of his fellow Catholics. He was ultimately arrested and spent some years in prison.

---

[17] The Maronites are a group of Eastern Catholics, named after their founder, Maro, and mainly settled in Lebanon.

When released, he cried out against 'traitors in Rome' who were co-operating with those who had been his oppressors. Ì still carry on my body the marks of the terror' he exclaimed to those who, like Pope Paul, were suddenly afflicted with deafness. The Pope, in fact, refused to recognise him as Patriarch; and from then on Slipyi encountered a surprising number of obstacles and harassments at every turn.

3.

It was only to be expected that the Vatican's attitude would, sooner or later, be reflected by a similar change of heart among the people of Rome; and elections held there in 1978 brought about a result that would once have been regarded as a catastrophe, but which now passed as commonplace. For the newly returned President was Sandro Pertini, a life-long member of the Communist Party who soon introduced measures that affected every sphere in the hitherto settled precincts of Italian family life.

Many Catholics, influenced by the friendly relationship that had existed between the Red leaders and Good Pope John, gave their votes to Pertini.

Traditionalists called to mind the directions given by the Marquis de Franquerie in *L'infaillibilité Pontificale* to those who were planning to infiltrate the Church: 'Let us popularise vice through the masses. Whatever their five senses strive after it shall be satisfied.... Create hearts full of vice and you will no longer have any Catholics.' And now, as the Marquis had rightly anticipated, a general breakdown occurred in every social grade and every department of life; from junior schools to factories, on the streets, and in the home.

Murders increased, as did the kidnapping of wealthy people who were held to ransom. Crime and chaos flourished as a barrage of anti-police propaganda weakened the law. The prevailing axiom, and not only among the young, was that anything goes.' Pornography flourished. The hammer and sickle emblem was painted on church doors, and scrawls ridiculing priests, the Church, and religion in general appeared on walls and hoardings.

The Pope's reaction to this did not surprise those who were already dismayed by his pro-Communist views. He invited Pertini to the Vatican, where, it was discovered, the two men had so much in common that their meeting was afterwards described by the Pope as having been emotional. 'The encounter brought us very close,' he said. 'The eminent visitor's words were simple, profound, and full of solicitude for the welfare of man, for all humanity.'

In the same year Giulio Argan became Mayor of Rome. He too was a hardened Communist, and his election provided further proof of the way in which the political pendulum was swinging in Italy. Pope Paul, expressing satisfaction with the turn of events, looked forward to working with the mayor in a spirit of 'desire, confidence, and anticipated gratitude.'

We have so far given instances of the Pope's personal commitment to Marxist principles. And that he was by no means averse to compromising with or surrendering the Church's doctrine was proved by the way he handled the case of Alighiero Tondi, a priest who left the Church and became an ardent worker for Moscow.

Tondi married Carmen Zanti, whom he chose as being the possessor of a melancholy look and a sweet voice.' Tondi had never been dispensed from his former vows, but Pope Paul had no difficulty in declaring that his marriage, void of any religious form, was canonically valid.

Meanwhile Carmen had used her voice to such good effect that she was elected to the Soviet Chamber of Deputies, and afterwards to the Senate. Then, both K.G.B. agents, they went to Berlin where Carmen, who was obviously more pushing than Tondi (who was experiencing qualms of conscience) became the leader of the Womens' Communist organisation.

Tondi, who never quite forgot his ordination, was suffering a premature dread of hell fire, and wished to return to the Church. Nothing could be easier, said the not-at-all squeamish Pope Paul. He removed the ban of excommunication from the penitent, assured him that he had no need to recant, and declared that his marriage was still perfectly valid.

The fact of Communism having been given à human face,' and by no less a legislator than the Head of the Church, was not without effect on other countries. When the National Committee of Catholic Action for Workers met in France, it was attended by seven card-carrying members of the Communist Party. The French Bishops overlooked their anti-national and disruptive tendencies.

In England, Cardinal Hume of Westminster expressed sympathy for movements that challenged the authority of governments opposed to the Left. And in February 1981, Cardinal Gray and his Auxiliary Bishop, Monsignor Monaghan, leaders of the Archdiocese of St. Andrews and Edinburgh, called on Catholics to support Amnesty International, a movement that, under the banner of Human Rights, gave what help it could, moral and otherwise, to agitators who, in several parts of the world, worked for the overthrow of established order.

Dissatisfied elements within the Church, who had weaker voices and no clenched fist to emphasise their protest, soon discovered that they had no right of appeal against the imposition of what, to them, was a more deadly danger than heresy. A spokesman for traditional Catholics in America, Father Gommar de Parrw, explained their bewilderment to the Vatican, and begged for guidance. His letter was not even acknowledged. When it was announced that a congress of Spanish priests, for the defence of the Mass, would be held at Saragossa, an edict issued by Pope Paul, at almost the last minute, prevented the meeting.

4.

The once proudly independent colours of the Catholic Church were hauled perceptibly lower when Pope Paul entered into 'dialogue' with the World Council of Churches.

At that time, 1975, more than two hundred and seventy religious organisations, of various kinds, were grouped under the Council, and it soon became clear that it stood for the liberation theories that had been introduced by John XXIII and since furthered by Paul VI. It had funds to spare for subversive movements in what is called the Third World, so that even our Press was forced to complain of the support it handed out.

Its gifts were not niggardly. For instance, as the Daily *Express* deplored, £45,000 had gone to terrorists who were responsible for the massacre of white women, children, and missionaries; and the Anglican *Church Times* remarked that the World Council of Churches 'has developed a political bias recognisably Marxist in its preference for a revolution of a Left-ward character.'

The Catholic Church had always stood apart from the World Council. But the advent of ecumenism had changed all that, and the Council's dangerous tendencies were made light of in order to foster harmony between the different religions.

Pope Paul, acclaimed as being always ready to move with the times, was willing to see eye to eye with the Council. But he had to move warily, as Catholic opinion throughout the world had, so far, been well trained to resist any encroachment upon its rights and its historical claim.

So when asked whether an alliance could be effected, he returned a diplomatic 'not yet.' But he showed where his sympathies were by following that up with a personal gift of £4,000 to further the Council's work and its aid to guerrillas.

The present Pope, John Paul II, has announced his intention of renewing negotiations with the pro-terrorists.

5.

There is a more sinister note on which to end this summary of Pope Paul's intransigence.

The name of a self-confessed devil worshipper, Cardonnel, is practically unknown here; but in other countries his writings excited a variety of feelings ranging from awed admiration to horror in those who read them.

As a member of the Dominican Order, he was given permission to speak in Paris Notre-Dame in mid-Lent 1968. Listeners were struck by his rabid anti-Christian expressions, on account of which he was called 'le theologian de la more Dieu' (the God's death theologian). He boasted of the title, left his Order and finally the Church, and became a hardened devil-worshipper. In a typical outburst he likened the Christian God to Stalin, to a beast, and finally to Satan.

Pope Paul admired his work; and although he ignored requests from Catholics who wished to safeguard their religion, he made a special point of writing to Cardonnel, congratulating him and sending good wishes.

Part Nine

O change beyond report, thought, or belief!

Milton.

The following section has been written with some misgivings. For on the one hand it leads up, in a subsequent part, to events that are startling, obscene, desecrating, which have taken place in buildings consecrated by ritual and by history, that the still practising Catholic may prefer to ignore. While on the other hand it deals with the Church's teaching on the Mass, or rather, on what the Church taught about the Mass when it still spoke with an authority that was recognised even by those who refused to accept it.

It is therefore necessary, to clear the understanding of those who may not have been acquainted with that teaching, to glance at a few essential aspects concerning it.

The Mass was not merely a service. It was the central act in the Church's life, a great mystery by which bread and wine were consecrated and so became the actual body and blood of Christ. It was the sacrifice of Calvary enacted over again, an earnest of the salvation effected by Christ who was there, under the sacred species of bread ('This is my Body') and wine, upon the altar.

Whenever a Catholic found himself in strange surroundings, the Mass was there as a rallying point for his worship. So it had been, with but a few minor alterations, for Latin Catholics from the earliest Christian centuries (beginning, roughly, from the seventh century) on record. And so it would remain, the Church taught and the faithful believed, until the end of time, a bulwark against error that inspired an air of sanctity-or impressive hanky-panky, call it what you will-that was recognised by devotee and disbeliever alike.

Typical of those who knew this was the Liberal and Protestant Augustine Birrell, 1850-1933, who was sometime Secretary for Ireland. 'It is the Mass that matters,' he said. 'It is the Mass that makes the difference, so hard to define, between a Catholic country and a Protestant one, between Dublin and Edinburgh.'

The unique quality of what may be called, in pedestrian terms, a landmark in religion, has always influenced the plans of those who set out to overcome the Church. The Mass has always stood in their path, a stumbling block that had to be demolished before their attack could make headway. It was denigrated as a base superstition, a mere operation of the hands, accompanied by words, that deceived the over-credulous.

The assault against it was heaviest, and partly successful, in the sixteenth century; and when the Church recovered its breath it called a Council that took its name from the little town of Trent, which later became an Italian province, where the principles of the counter-Reformation were defined. And those principles took shape, largely, as a defence of the focal point that had never been lost sight of-the Mass.

It was codified by Pius V, the future saint who had started life as a shepherd boy and who, in keeping with Rome's verdict that Henry VIII's marriage to Anne Boleyn had been invalid, declared that their child, the English Queen Elizabeth I, was therefore both heretic and bastard. And from then on the echoes of his firm, uncompromising yet always dignified thunder had lived on in association with the old Romanesque cathedral of Trent, the place that gives its name, Tridentine, to the order of the Mass that was intended to pass into general use for the whole Church, and for all time.

The Missal he drew up, and in which this was decreed, leaves no doubt as to that: At no time in the future can a priest ever be forced to use any other way of saying Mass. And in order once for all to preclude any scruples of conscience and fear of ecclesiastical penalties and censures, we declare herewith that it is by virtue of our Apostolic authority that we decree and prescribe that this present order of ours is to last in perpetuity and never at a future date can it be revoked or legally amended.'

The decree specifically warned All persons in authority, of whatever dignity or rank, Cardinals not excluded, and to command them as a matter of strict obedience never to use or permit any ceremonies and Mass prayers other than those contained in this Missal.'

This was repeated, as though to make doubly clear even to those who were already converted, that he was speaking as Pope: Ànd so this Council reaches the true and genuine doctrine about this venerable and divine Sacrifice of the Eucharist-the doctrine which the Catholic Church has always held, and which She will hold until the end of the world, as She learned it from Christ Our Lord Himself, from the Apostles, and from the Holy Ghost.'

Few Papal assertions have been more explicit. The Mass, as generally known, was to be preserved, unaltered and unalterable, for all time. But Cardinal Bugnini, who had gone on clinging to the office after his membership of a secret society had become known, and Paul VI, who affected to be unaware of any such revelation, made short work of Pope St. Pius V's pronouncement.

It later became known that some twenty years before Vatican Two made pulp of the traditional Mass book, a priest-professor had been detailed to draw up plans for gradual liturgical changes; while in December 1963 the Council introduced new practices and a new phraseology that, at first, made little impact on the public.

But now Pope Paul and Cardinal Bugnini, assisted by Cardinal Lercaro, went straight ahead, with the assistance of non-Catholics whom they called 'authoritative experts of sacred theology.'

2.

The experts called in to amend the Most Holy Sacrament of the Catholic Church comprised one or two Protestants; Canon Ronald Jasper; Robert McAfee Brown, a Presbyterian; Biother Thurion, who was a Lutheran; a Calvinist, a Rabbi, and a certain Joachim Jeremias, a one-time Professor of Gottingen University who denied the divinity of Christ.

Bugnini said that they were merely present as observers, that they had no voice when the changes were discussed. But apart from the fact that they claimed to have played an active part in the Concilium, that they commented upon it and made suggestions, one need only ask-why, without some set purpose, were they ever invited to participate?

Whatever this very mixed bag decided, said Pope Paul, would be 'in accordance with God's will.' It was also intended to correspond to the temper of 'modern man.' And what emerged from their deliberations was a Novus *Ordo* (New Mass) missal, a veritable sign of the times which meant that the era of a 'MiniMass,' and of 'pop' music in Church, with all the profanities it led to, was about to begin.

Such innovations extracted a blind obedience from those who believed that conformity to whatever was said and done by the priesthood, especially in church, was a virtue. Some who questioned the changes were told not to presume any further. It was said to be contumacious, and displeasing to God; while the fact that many were resolute in opposing the changes, and turned their backs upon the Novus *Ordo*, called forth the charge that they were in mortal sin, and inflicting another wound on the loving Father who was waiting to welcome them.

After all, the Vatican and its spokesman-in-chief, Pope Paul, had approved the changes. A revolution had been achieved, and it was all for the good. The old Roman Missal had become a back number. The progressives were cock-a-hoop. And now they proceeded to pass beyond their original objective and pressed forward.

A number of what may at first appear to be minor practices came under their scrutiny.

Genuflecting, and kneeling to receive Holy Communion, were found to be unnecessary. One entering a church, the interior of which had long been familiar, suffered a shock when it was seen that the perhaps priceless Travertine altar had been replaced by a table, at which the priest, who was now sometimes called the president, faced the people and, in a clumsy vernacular instead of the old verbal music (for Latin has always been hated by the enemies of the Church) invited the congregation to join in are past.'

The manner of receiving Communion now differed greatly. The Host might be given into the hand, as was evidenced when Pope Paul celebrated a New Mass at Geneva. A number of Hosts were passed to a girl who was standing conveniently near, and these she distributed into the hands, sometimes grubby or sticky, of those about her, or into the hand of any chance looker-on who came up to see what was being given away.

Another method was to place the one-time Sacred Elements in a chalice and then invite the people to come forward and help themselves. An extra relish could be given to the bread by dunking it in the wine. It had hitherto been out of the question for non-Catholics to receive Communion at Mass. But Pope Paul introduced a new 'updating' by permitting a self-confessed Presbyterian lady, Miss Barberina Olsen, to receive the wafer.

His example was followed. First Cardinal Bea, and after him Cardinal Willebrands, empowered their Bishops to issue an open invitation; and then Cardinal Suenens, at the close of a Congress at Medellion, in Columbia, called on all and sundry to come forward with open mouth or ready hand.

A more decisive battle was fought out in Rome, where Bugnini's New Mass was celebrated in the Sistine Chapel. A large majority of the prelates who were present voted against it. The actual numbers were seventy-eight in favour, two hundred and seven against. The orthodox Cardinal Ottaviani, who never lost caste, examined the text of the vandalised version, and found that it contained some twenty heresies.

'The New Mass,' he said, 'departs radically from Catholic doctrine and dismantles all defences of the Faith.' The same sentiment was expressed by Cardinal Heenan of Westminster: 'The old boast that the Mass is everywhere the same ... is no longer true.'

Ottaviani was head of the Holy Office, which exercised guardianship over faith and morals.

Pope Paul clamped down upon the office, and clipped the Cardinal's claws; and he was so annoyed by the adverse vote that he forbade the New Mass ever to be the subject of a ballot again. From then on it was given official, but not popular sanction. Thousands of people, who would not tolerate a form of the Mass that was less dignified than the Protestant Communion service, either left or stopped going to church. Many priests followed suit. Those who stood by the incontrovertible ruling of Pius V on the Mass were threatened with suspension, or even excommunication.

One of the first to be declared anathema, for observing the old Mass, was a priest who was somewhat remote from the scenes of tension, a Father Carmona of Acapulco, in Mexico. Bishop Ackermann of Covington, America, when faced with a number of orthodox and therefore recalcitrant priests in his diocese, lamented helplessly 'What can I do? I can't throw them into jail.' Their doubts were embodied in a question that was left for Pope Paul to answer-whether the introduction of the New Mass was the beginning of an age of new darkness on the earth, or the harbinger of an unprecedented crisis within the Church?

He refused to answer. And the same wall of silence was encountered by a deputation of priests who begged for a return to the traditional. Mass; while thousands from several parts of Europe, who went to Rome with the same purpose in mind, were turned away.

Those who brought about the changes had not been working blindly. They had followed a plan, in conformance with the secret design that furnishes the theme of these pages. They now had the future in their hands, and the confident way in which they accepted this was made clear by an article in *L'Osservatore Romano,* which depicted the pretty hopeless future awaiting those priests who braved the wrath of the Vatican by carrying out the duties for which they had been trained.

They would, said the article, become headless, autonomous priests facing an arid, squalid life. No sheltered future, no promotion to the hierarchy, no expectation of a pension at the end of their ministry.'

One who had been most zealous in promoting the changes sang their praises in the following terms: It is a different liturgy of the Mass. We want to say it plainly. The Roman rite as we knew it exists no more. It has gone. Some walls of the structure have fallen, others have been altered. We can look at it now as a ruin or as the particular foundation of a new building. We, must not weep over ruins or dream of an historical reconstruction. Open new ways, or we shall be condemned as Jesus condemned the Pharisees.'[18]

Pope Paul was equally extreme in approving the findings of the Second Vatican Council's commission on the Liturgy: 'The old rite of the Mass is in fact the expression of a warped ecclesiology.'

---

[18] Father Joseph Gelineau. *The Liturgy-Today and Tomorrow.* (Darton, Longman, and Todd, 1978.)

Reading that, some may have been reminded of the old Coronation Oath, that ran as follows:[19]

I vow to change nothing of the received tradition, and nothing thereof I found before me guarded by my God-pleasing predecessors, to encroach, to alter, or permit any innovation therein.

'To the contrary; with glowing affection to reverently safeguard the passed on good, with my whole strength and my utmost effort. 'To cleanse all that is in contradiction with canonical order that may surface.

'To guard the whole canons and decrees of our Popes likewise as divine ordinances of heaven, because I am conscious of Thee, whose place I take through the grace of God.

'If I should undertake to act in anything of contrary sense, or permit that it will be executed, Thou willst not be merciful to me on the dreadful day of Divine Justice.

'Accordingly, without exclusion, we subject to severest excommunication anyone-be it myself or be it another-who would dare to undertake anything new in contradiction to this constituted evangelical tradition and the purity of the orthodox Faith and the Christian religion, or would seek to change anything by his opposing efforts, or would concur with those who undertake such blasphemous venture.'

Whenever this oath may have been taken at the time of a coronation, I know not. But its principles, until the Roncalli era, were tacitly accepted and endorsed as a conventional part of Papal observance.

For instance, one of the greatest and most gifted of the Popes, Pius II (1458-64) in his Bull *Execrabilis*, repeated a law that was endorsed through the centuries and accepted, without modification, by what has always been referred to as the

---

[19] Translated by Dr. Werner Henzellek from *Vatican II, Reform Council or constitution of a new Church? By* Anton Holzer.

magisterium of the Church: 'Any Council called to make drastic change in the Church is beforehand decreed to be void and annulled.'

But Paul VI, the friend of Communists, who collaborated with the anarchist Alinsky and with the Mafia gangster, Sindona, issued his own statement of policy which appeared in *L'Osservatore Romano*, on April the 22nd, 1971, English edition:

'We moderns, men of our own day, wish everything to be new. Our old people, the traditionalists, the conservatives, measured the value of things according to their enduring quality.

We, instead, are actualists, we want everything to be new all the time, to be expressed in a continually improvised and dynamic unusual form.

It was raving of this sort (reminiscent of 'Peter Simple's' sarcasm in *The Daily Telegraph*) that led to the introduction of eatables such as roast beef, jellies, and hot dogs, washed down by draughts of coca-cola, in the Holy Sacrifice of the Mass, and to nuns clicking their heels and twisting their bodies, in a kind of *carmagnole*, to mark the Offertory.

'Anti-Christ,' said Hilaire Belloc in 1929, 'will be a man.'

But perhaps the most ludicrous justification of the change was put forward by one of our most 'progressive' Bishops, who said to the present writer: 'The New Mass got off to a ringing start yesterday. The guitars were going all over my diocese.'

3.

The doctrinal and liturgical changes in the Church were not long in showing the effects that the conservatives had forecast; and startling though many of them were, they still remain largely unknown even to people who live in the countries where they occurred.

It used to be looked back upon as an outrage of the most extreme order when, during the French Revolution, a harlot was hoisted on to the altar of Notre Dame where she was crowned and worshipped as the Goddess of Reason; or when Chartres Cathedral was on the point of being converted into a Temple of Reason.

But such things pale into insignificance when compared with the desecrations and obscenities that have taken place, often with the approval of prelates, in some of the most revered Catholic minsters on both sides of the Atlantic.

There was a marked falling off from established ritual when such things as a communal supper took the place of a solemn Mass; when the priest, armed with a bread knife, had a large loaf placed in front of him which he proceeded to cut into chunks, helping the others and then himself until a general munching of jaws showed their appreciation of the Body of Christ. Such suppers, served in a parishioner's house, became a regular feature of Dutch family life. Sometimes the 'lady of the house,' instead of a priest, officiated at Mass that was served in her 'best room.'

There were not a few places where the traditional office of priest was taken over by a woman, who walked among the congregation giving out the Sacrament to any who stood with gaping mouth and a nauseous display of tongue and teeth. Sometimes it was placed in the sweaty hand of a child, or between the trembling fingers and palm of a geriatric who promptly dropped it on the floor, where it could be trampled; or it might be self-administered.

One small girl came away from Mass, in one of the more 'advanced' quarters of Holland, saying that she had learnt more there than she ever had through seeing her brother in a bath. For the altar-boy who, in England, would have passed for a fourth former, had been naked.

Pope Paul, determined not to lag behind in the scurry for progress, signed a special edict whereby any who cared to help themselves to the Blood of Christ could suck it up through a straw. In that way some churches came to resemble a coffee bar, especially when the blare of a discotheque issued from the sanctuary, together with the shouting, strumming, and stamping of feet that accompany the celebration of a jazz Mass, a beat, and a 'yeah-yeah' Mass. There were teenage Masses where, instead of the sacramental Bread and Wine, hot dogs, buns, and coca-cola were served. At others, whisky and cream crackers took the place of the elements. Some priests found the wearing of an alb inconvenient when saying Mass, and so resorted to shirt-sleeves.

The new freedom offered a chance for political extremists to advertise their usually Left-wing tenets. One of the foremost seminaries in Canada was sold to Chinese Reds, who tore out the tabernacle and put in its place a portrait of the wholesale murderer Mao Tse Tung. It later became a training centre for revolutionary street fighters.

In September, 1971, the Catholic school at Vald'Or, Abitibi, Quebec, initiated a new game for boys. It consisted of spitting at the figure of Christ on the cross, and the one who covered the face with the biggest spit was declared winner. This was reported in the French-Canadian paper, *Vers Demain*, in September, 1971.

In one South American province, where disturbances rarely died down, a local Bishop Casaldaliga came out on the side of the Russian-inspired insurgents. He adopted the rough and ready garb of a guerrilla, complete with cartridge belt, and went on preaching and officiating at Mass under the name he gave himself, Monsignor Hammer and Sickle.

But a truly sinister scene was enacted at the basilica of St. Maria de Guadelupe in Mexico City, where a goat was sacrificed in front of the high altar. Now it is not only the fact of an animal being killed, and in church, that excites comment. It seems to have called for none from the people there present who gaped, were astonished, and then walked away no doubt concluding that it was all part of the new order within the Church. And so it was. But Archbishop Gomez, who had charge of the basilica, knew more than that, as did the strange crowd of people to whom he actually rented it for the occasion.

The goat, said to have been created by the Devil, figures in the Satanic lore of those whose secret design has always been the downfall of the Church. The happening referred to resembles part of the old pre-Christian ritual, when a goat was sacrificed at an altar during the Day of Atonement. The sins of the High Priest, and of the people, were transferred to a second animal of the same species, which then became the scapegoat and was driven into the wilderness; or, in demonology, it was forced over a cliff into the hell-fire that was tended by Azazel, a fallen angel.

Hence it was no ordinary Mass but a Black Mass that was celebrated in Mexico City, with the use of an inverted cross, an event that was filmed and recorded by those who arranged it.

But such things marked only a beginning, as did a growing clamour, supported by priests, for abortion, and for sexual aberrations to be recognized as perfectly normal. There were priests who almost shouted from the housetops that they were glad to be homosexual, as it was a privilege that conferred the psychological fulfilment of one's personality.' It became accepted, in some parts, for perverts of the same sex to be married in church.

In Paris, a man and a woman, minus every stitch of clothing, paraded their nakedness before an altar, where they were married by a priest who conveyed to them what has been called the sublime' nuptial blessing. Advanced Holland, not to be outdone, reacted with the news that a couple of male homos had exchanged vows and tokens in a church wedding; while an American priest, who was still holding on despite the fact that he had been cited in a divorce case, gleefully smote his breast and affirmed that he too was an emancipated moral pervert, which he afterwards ratified by uniting a pair of lesbians in matrimony.

It was a fruitful time for cranks and opportunists of every kind. An ex-nun, Rita Mary, joined an American lay community whose members were committed to the new spirit emerging in religious life.' A breath from that spirit of newness suddenly revealed to her that 'God the Father is female.' Others who favoured the cause of women's liberation adopted the same slogan, and as part of their campaign cars adorned with stickers exhorting people to Pray to God, she will provide,' appeared on the streets.

Traders were quick to seize upon it as a good stunt, and Rita Mary's vehicles were soon joined by others offering a more material tip: 'With Jesus on your side you can be a more successful businessman.'

Still keeping to America, there was a gathering at Stubenville, Ohio, in July 1976, at which a thousand priests endorsed a novel intention to de-clericalise the ministry,' which meant, in effect, putting themselves out of work. They were advised to get ready for the collapse of the social order; then, after prayers, some discovered that they had been given the gift of healing. A general laying on of hands followed, and from that the mixed congregation, amid shouting, fell to hugging and kissing each other.

Bursts of spontaneous affection, as we shall see, were fast becoming a feature of the New Mass, as also was a growing obsession with sex. The exploration of touch,' referring to bodies, became a new kind of worship.

At a meeting in Philadelphia, where Cardinal Wright and eight of his Bishops were present, the main speaker, Father Gallagher, told his audience that 'touching is crucial.' And it may be assumed that many suppressed instincts found a relief that had long been clamoured for in the words that followed: 'Do not hold hands sexlessly.' The nine prelates conveyed smiles and blessings to the love in,' as such displays of emotion were coming to be called, that followed.

A variation on the same theme was heard at the National Pastoral Congress at Liverpool in 1980, where a declaration was passed that, much to the surprise of a representative English audience, deified the most taken-for-granted of their marital acts: 'During sexual intercourse a man and his wife create Christ:' a statement that sounds suspiciously like Aleister Crowley's words, that 'sexual organs are the image of God.'

The latest excursion into the realm of ecclesiastical nonsense (January, 1982) has been made by Bishop Leo McCartie, the Catholic Auxiliary Bishop of Birmingham. Let Rastafarians, he urged, the mostly young blacks who wear woolly caps and plait their hair into strings, be given the use of church premises. They worship the late Emperor Haile Selassie of Ethiopia as the true god, they believe that Christ was black, and they smoke cannabis as part of their religious ritual.

The Bishop admits that the Church could not condone the smoking of cannabis on its premises, *but only because it is against the* law (my emphasis). But Rastafarianism, he goes on, is a valid religious experience, and its followers use cannabis like a sacrament, 'which is comparable to the chalice or communion cup in Christian worship.' So now we know.

Let us take a few more instances of what the modernistic trend has achieved in America, all, let it be remembered, without calling forth more than an isolated protest, here and there, from any of the hierarchy. Moreover it was all approved by Pope Paul as was shown by the presence of his official representative who passed on Papal greetings to those who dressed up, cavorted, and made irreligious idiots of themselves to demonstrate the new freedom.

For the past two years, on June the 28th, St. Patrick's Cathedral, New York, has been the finishing point of what is known, to ecclesiastical and secular authorities alike, as a Gay Parade.

In 1981 an estimated crowd of 50,000 marched up Fifth Avenue, led by a figure with a whitened face, and wearing a frilly ankle-length dress and a bonnet, who spun up and down the road and pavement in front of the cathedral on roller-skates. At least one of the lookers-on recognised the figure as being that of a reputable Wall Street broker.

An individual who was hailed as the Grand Marshal of the Parade then stepped from a black limousine, performed clown-like on the steps then, delicately holding a bouquet of pansies, made as if to enter the front door. By that time a Mr. McCauley, who practised as a New York attorney, already sickened by what he had seen, snatched the flowers and threw them in the faces of those who swarmed after the Marshal. A scuffle broke out, and police led the objector away.

It took two hours for the parade to pass a given point and gather about the cathedral. Some were dressed as priests, others were nuns; some were wearing black leather and chains. There was a group called Dignity, and another known as the North American Man-Boy Love Association.

They carried a large sign announcing that 'Man-Boy Love is Beautiful,' the older members walking armin-arm with boys, whose average age was about thirteen, and some of whom wore bathing suits.

The Gay Socialists carried a red banner, and shouted their hatred of God and the Church as they marched. But their frenzy was more than matched by that of the Gay Militant Atheists, who roared in unison: 'Smash the Church! Death to the Church!' Another cry of 'Smash the State!' showed that the real driving power behind the demonstration was making itself heard.

Then came an interlude as a male, in a nun's habit and trailing a cross upside down, executed a dance, accompanied by obscene gestures, for a full half-hour. That was followed by a group that came forward and made as if to light a candle at the cathedral door. By then Mr. McCauley had returned. He renewed his protest, asked the police to stop the outrageous performances, and was promptly arrested.

The homosexuals then proceeded to drape a large banner about the barricades they had erected at the front steps of the cathedral. A captain of the City Fire Department then came forward and asked a police officer to intervene. The officer turned his back, whereupon the Fire Chief seized the banner, rolled it up and threw it on the ground.

The yelling mob swarmed over him. He was pulled down, his jacket was torn from his back, blows rained upon him, his fingers were seized and bent in an effort to break them, his legs were forced apart and hands reached for and grabbed his genitals. When he could speak, he told the police officer that he wished to press charges against those who had attacked him. The policeman sneered. 'Come back tomorrow at the same time and see if you can recognise them.' When the Fire Chief persisted, the policeman gripped his revolver so tightly and menacingly that his knuckles were seen to whiten.

Only two people were arrested, Mr. McCauley and the Fire Chief, both for disorderly conduct.

They later heard the charges against them being framed. One police official said: 'Say that you saw him assault someone.' Another said: 'Put in that he broke through the police line.'

Meanwhile the parade was going on, with the cathedral front being emblazoned with provocative signs and banners, one announcing that 'Jesus was a homosexual.' Doggerel was chanted. 'Two, four, six, eight. Do you know if your kids are straight?' Finally a flag was hung from the cathedral door. It was designed like the American flag, except that in place of the stars, sex symbols and representations of the penis were substituted.

The demonstrators, followed by a large crowd; made their way to Central Park, where they engaged in a free-for-all public exhibition of sex acts. Frightened people who had gone to the cathedral in search of consolation or quiet bunched together throughout the afternoon in side chapels and corners. When approached on the matter, the members of the Diocesan Curia said there had been nothing to complain about.

In Virginia, a priest drove a Volkswagen down the aisle of his church to mark Christ's entry into Jerusalem. Later he had a fork1~ift placed in the churchyard and climbed into its basket, where he stood waving his arms while being lifted up to commemorate Ascension Day. In Boston, Massachusetts, priests attired as clowns, with red hearts decorating their foreheads, scrambled and jostled about a church trying to catch balloons. A priest wearing a singlet and jeans cavorted in church with a girl whose flesh bulged from her leotard.

In this country, one Sunday evening, television went out of its way to show an Auxiliary Bishop processing up the aisle of one of our Catholic cathedrals. He was led to the altar by a young girl who danced and skipped about in front of him like a young horse. The celebration of Holy Mass in another church concluded with the singing of 'For he's a jolly good fellow.'[20]

Similar outbreaks occurred even in Latin countries, where the mysteries of the Church had long been part of the national consciousness, its blood and bone. For visitors to a church near Grenoble, in the Isere department of France, on a day in 1970, were surprised to see that the ornaments and candlesticks were being removed from the altar, and that the space before it was cleared. Then ropes were put in place to form a business-like representation of a ring where, according to the bills, an international boxing contest was to take place.

At the appointed time, a throng that was far from typical of the usual one seen there, and mostly male, shuffled, stumbled, or made their way arrogantly into the building where some of them had been baptised, and some married. As they acquired a more familiar feeling odds were shouted and bets made, but details of the fight were never recorded.

Whether it was won on points, or 6y a knock-out; who acted as referee or time-keeper, and who plied the sponges; how much the church funds profited from the purse or the takings, none of this

---

[20] *The Sunday Telegraph.* February 21st, 1982.

appears in the parish register. Neither does a protest from the Bishop.

On a Friday in early December, 1974, the coronation church of France, Rheims Cathedral, was given over to a horde of hippies and lay-abouts for one of their all-night sessions. The Archbishop and his clergy, who had obligingly provided the setting, may have noted, with a feeling of envy, as the prematurely aged youth of the district poured in, that they far exceeded in number those who were seen at High Mass on Sundays and Holy Days.

Cacophony was provided by the Tangerine Orange Group, and when the mixed congregation grew tired of waving their arms and shuffling in time to the uproar, they settled down to an orgy of drugs and hashish smoking.

When this affair became known, angry parishioners demanded that the Cathedral, which occupies a special place in history, should undergo a service of purification.

But their protests were waved aside by Father Bernard Goreau, who held the always questionable post of 'cultural attaché' of the archdiocese. He agreed that the dancers and smokers had been left to their own devices for hours in the Gothic darkness. 'But,' he added, 'things might have been worse.'

Indeed they might. We are told that they only urinated and copulated on the stone floor ... over which the Kings of old France had passed on the way to their anointing, and where Joan of Arc, holding her blazon, had stood like a soldier home from the war.

Also in France, it was not unknown for a priest to light and smoke a cigarette while saying Mass.

Even Rome was not immune from the sacrilegious parodies that followed the new religious freedom, the opening of the windows of the Church. The scene of one, in 1975, was the classroom of a Roman convent. Pope Paul was present, but the star turn was provided by Fred Ladenius, a gentleman from the Middle West who had acquired celebrity through appearing on Belgian television. He had furthermore been spoken of by an enthusiast as 'the born again spirit, whose God updated the Jesus of 1974 by being the God of 1975.'[21]

Fred set about his task right manfully, stripping off his jacket and giving voice to almost incoherent ravings for which, he said, he was in no way responsible. What they heard were some of the truths he-had received, that very morning, from the Lord's mouth. For the Lord spoke and prophesied through him. Fred accompanied these revelations by flinging up his arms so violently that he broke into a sweat. But he was by no means exhausted. He rolled up his shirt-sleeves and invited all those who wished to receive the Lord, to come up 'rapido.'

Fred, though still in a state of undiminished perspiration, waved his hands frantically over the heads of those who accepted the invitation, and accompanied each gesture with a cry of 'Hallelujah!' At the end of these ministrations the school blackboard was moved to make way for a table, on which were placed two chalices, one holding wine, and the other wafers of the kind that are used to celebrate Mass.

Then everyone fell into line and followed the example of Fred, who took out a wafer and dipped it in the wine before transferring it to his mouth. The meeting broke up amid more and louder cries of 'Hallelujah!' in which the Pope joined, and with further manifestations that the spirit was indeed moving amongst them.

Fred was duly rewarded by being sent for by the Pope, who thanked him warmly for all the good work he was doing for the Church. Fred stayed on in Rome, where he acted for a time as the Vicar of Christ's Press Secretary.

In the Church's calendar, one year in every twenty-five is declared to be a Holy Year. It is a time of special pilgrimages,

---

[21] For more details of this and other events in Rome see *From Rome, Urgently* (Stratimari, Rome) by Mary Martinez, a lively book to which I am much indebted. I have also drawn upon another eye-witness account by Louise Marciana, formerly a Sister of the Precious Blood. It was at that Order's convent that some of the antics here described took place.

when millions do penance to mark their adherence to the Faith and to obtain what is called the Great Pardon. Throughout that time Rome is seething with visitors from every part of the world, and on the last occasion of a Holy Year being declared, in 1975, Pope Paul extended a welcome, couched in the terms of emancipated religion to the new generation who had come in search of a liberating and inspiring aid, in search of a new word, a new ideal.'

Those who attended High Mass in St. Peter's on May the 19th, half-way through Holy Year, in expectation of those spiritual advantages, were in no way disappointed. They numbered some ten thousand. Cardinal Suenens officiated at the high altar. Pope Paul was present. Five hundred priests were ranged about them. This is how an experienced Catholic journalist described what happened when the time came to receive Holy Communion:[22]

'It was not uncommon to see what one first thought of as white petals being scattered among the congregation. Only when I could push my way nearer did I realise that they were handfuls of consecrated Hosts, that the Cardinal's hench-priests were scattering among the crowd.... They fell on the shoulders of men, on the dyed and coverless heads of women, and as was inevitable, not a few fell on the ground and were trampled upon by the crowd.

I spoke to a lady standing near me who was gobbling a number of them together. I asked her where she came from and was she a Catholic. She came from Egypt, she replied, and in fact had no religious persuasion, but her feelings were in favour of Mohammedanism.'

Tape-recorders were held high above the assembly, that was fast being galvanised into a state of excitement. Suddenly a voice boomed out through a microphone placed near the altar that God was not only present but was now, in fact, actually speaking,

---

[22] Simon Keegan. *News-Letter of the International Priests Association.* Published by St. George's Presbytery, Polegate, East Sussex.

albeit in a strong and nasal American accent-one wonders whether the ubiquitous Fred was in action again?

Then Pope Paul took up the running. He gathered up handfuls of Hosts, pressed them upon people whose mouths were already full of the consecrated species, so that they could only free their hands by passing the Hosts on to others, who either crumpled them up or dropped them on the floor. The Pope, beginning to give an address, had to raise his voice in order to be heard above the growing turmoil, to which he added by exclaiming a further anachronistic 'Hallelujah!' and flinging up his arms.

By now some of the people were dancing. Others squatted or huddled on the floor among the trodden fragments of what, those same people had been taught, was the body of Christ. They swayed in time to a low moaning, an expression of the ecstasy inspired by the occasion, that grew in volume until it filled the basilica.

Still in the same year, a visitor to the church of St. Ignatius, in the street that bears the name of the founder of the Jesuits, in Rome, would have noticed that a heavy curtain was covering the main altar. Moreover, the seats had been turned round, as though to indicate that those who attended the service did not wish to be reminded of the lapis lazuli urn containing the relics of St. Aloysius Gonzaga.

A battery of microphones and loud-speakers was in evidence, and through one of these the voice of an Irish-American Jesuit, Father Francis Sullivan, was heard announcing, in the approved style of a follower of General Booth, that they had come together in order to praise the Lord. He went on to hammer home the fact that religion was in a state of flux, that everything was changing, and that it was a waste of time to take a nostalgic look back at things that used to be believed. His statements met with the smiling approval of Cardinal Suenens, who could always be relied on to patronise 'way out' effusions.

By now the Romans were getting used to having their faith supervised by oracles from the States; and they listened attentively when a second voice, from the same place of origin as Father Sullivan's, exhorted them to love one another. People who were packing the church, thus encouraged, began to use their eyes, exchange looks, and to sidle alongside the person of their choice. Did they imagine, the voice went on, that the gift of love was a privilege intended for the early Church only? Of course it wasn't!

With that, cries of agreement nearly split the roof, and couples fell into each other's arms, sprawling on the floor, arms and legs flailing, fingers and mouths giving vent to a passion that was no longer fearsomely restrained by their surroundings, but which could now find expression in a freedom akin to that known to lovers in a ditch. Those who were barred, by age or infirmity, from taking part in the spectacle, savoured it with a lickerish look, or danced a few steps, or sang the praises of the Host whose house they had turned into a Bedlam. Hallelujah! God was good, and all this showed that churchgoing could now be a joyous event.

At the height of the uproar, a friar in the brown garb of St. Francis of Assisi somehow managed to make himself heard. He was in dire physical straits, aware of a strange, mystical, and maternal sensation. He felt exactly as Mary had done when conceiving the Son. Full of grace... more applause... and Hallelujah again.

What was left of St. Aloysius in his urn remained silent, as also did St. Ignatius who, as a soldier, had known the cleanly hiss of a sword as it was drawn from its scabbard.

For the sake of providing a still more startling climax, let us look back to the year 1970, when a Progressive Theological Congress was held in a Franciscan church in Brussels. The principle subject discussed, in flat contradiction of the Congress's programme as indicated by its title, was sex, and it was expounded to an almost exclusively youthful gathering.

It was rightly anticipated, because of the theme, that Cardinal Suenens would be present; apart from which, as Primate of Belgium, he was on his home ground.

The Congress opened with the entry of girls, dressed in white and, as they twisted this way and that, waving cords and bits of broken chain to show that they were free. In an interval after the dancing, pieces of bread and glasses of wine were passed round, followed by grapes and cigarettes.

Then, just as the young conference members thought all was over, their eyes were drawn towards the altar from which something was beginning to rise and to take on an unbelievable shape.[23]

It was at first greeted with gasps, then giggles, and finally pandemonium broke loose as the transparent plastic forming the shape was seen to represent a gigantic penis. The delegates screamed themselves hoarse, feeling that it was a challenge to-a recognition of-their virility. It was the sort of climax that had never been imagined and might only figure in the most extravagant of bawdy dreams. The presence of the Cardinal gave a permissive glamour to a setting that they would never again regard with awe.

It is well in place here, as part of our thesis, to look somewhat more closely at the scene that occurred in the Brussels church, and at the word Hallelujah, which has never been in everyday use, as a *spoken* expression of praise, within the Seven Hills. As an offering of praise to Jehovah, it has always been commonly used by religious revivalists rather than by Latins. But now we find Pope Paul using it.

What made him? And why did Cardinal Suenens, before an altar, preside over an amazing exhibition of carnal tomfoolery that many, especially the church-bound, will find difficult or impossible to believe?

There is one explanation. Neither of those named, while wearing the robes, vestments, and all the outward signs of Catholic prelacy, were Christian men. They had passed, by preparatory stages, into the highest echelon of occult understanding. They had been tutored, signed for, and guaranteed by the Masters of

---

[23] Report from the Belgian News Service, quoted in *Il Giornale d'Italia*, September 17th, 1970.

Wisdom in one of the foremost temples where atavistic rites, all with sexual undertones, take the place of religion.

When the adolescent girls shrieked with delighted embarrassment as the large plastic penis rose up before them, Cardinal Suenens knew perfectly well that they were, as he intended, commemorating the heathen god Baal whose name, divided into its Sumerian[24] root words, has several meanings. Among them are lord, master, possessor, or husband, while others refer to a controlling male's penis with its forceful boring and thrusting.

So what the Cardinal arranged for the young, mostly girls, of Brussels, was a show of phallic worship, which symbolises the generative power contained in the semen, or life juice, which streamed down upon all life and nature from the mighty penis of Baal. An exaggerated phallus was also a symbol of Yesed, the sphere of the moon, and also of the horned god Dionysius, or Bacchus.

The praise chant voiced by Pope Paul has its origin in the same fount of heathen worship, as its meaning, again according to its Sumerian construct, refers to the strong water of fecundity, or semen. During the public displays of mass sexual intercourse, which go by the name of fertility rites, this semen, when ejaculated, was caught in the hands of the officiating priests, who held it up for the approval of Yahweh (Jehovah) and then proceeded to smear it upon their bodies.

So much was implied by Pope Paul when he raised his arms and uttered a heart-felt Hallelujah!

---

[24] From Sumer, which was a part of Babylonia.

Part Ten

One is always wrong to open a conversation with the Devil, for however he goes about it, he always insists on having the last word.

Andre Gide.

It is hoped that possible readers of this book, who may not be acquainted with the Catholic story, will by now have grasped one essential fact-that the general decline of the Church was brought about by the Council that goes by the name of Vatican Two. Furthermore, that the Council was called by John XXIII who, like several of the prelates and many of lesser title under his Papal wing, were clandestine members of secret societies, and who were, according to the age-long ruling of the Church, excommunicate and therefore debarred from fulfilling any legitimate priestly function. The disastrous results of their being allowed to do so, with Papal approbation (since both the Popes who followed Pius XII were part of the over-all conspiracy, while the recent John Paul I and John Paul II are subject to suspicion) are apparent to the most superficial observer. Such results are the outcome of Paul VI's main wish regarding the implementation of Vatican II, as expressed in his last will and testament, and repeated more than once by John Paul II: 'Let its prescriptions be put into effect.'

Those prescriptions were defined years- ago in the policies of Adam Weishaupt, Little Tiger, Nubius, and others (already quoted) for their trained disciples to infiltrate, and then to wear down the authority, practices, and very life of the Church. This they have accomplished, under the guise of progress or liberation.

Every aspect of the Church, spiritual and material, has been taken over, from Peter's Chair, with its once regal dignity, to a faldstool in the most insignificant parish church. The few priests who recognised this were kept in the background, or, if they managed to get a hearing, were exposed to ridicule; and surveying the scene, with its disorders, the exhibitions of profanity, and sexual aberrations staged in some of its most revered buildings, including St. Peter's, one is tempted to think of a once highly disciplined Guards brigade being transformed into a mob of screaming hooligans.

One may pass from the truism, that little things are little things, to a more comprehensive realisation that little beginnings are not little things; and it is by working precisely on that principle that the modern controllers of the Church achieved their ends without producing too much alarm among the populace at large.

They began by relaxing formal disciplines and inhibitions, such as keeping Friday as a meatless day. Then certain symbols, rituals, and devotions went. The old liturgical language of Latin practically disappeared. The nun's habit, which had never failed to inspire respect even in the most irreligious, went out of use, as did the cassock. The latter was sometimes replaced by jeans, as was demonstrated by two novices who, in Rome, went up to the altar to receive the blessing of their Father-General looking more like hippies than future Jesuits. A small cross, worn in the lapel of a jacket, was fast becoming the only sign that the wearer was a priest.

The old idea of priestly authority, whether exercised by a simple cleric or by the Pope, was effectively destroyed; and voices were always ready to applaud whenever the Church squandered this or that of its inheritance. 'The priest is today no longer a special being,' cried the exultant Yves Marsaudon, a member of the Masonic Supreme Council of France. A congress of moral theologians, held at Padua, went much further: 'The individual conscience is the Christian's supreme authority above the Papal magisterium.'

It was becoming generally accepted that one day the traditional Church must disappear or adapt itself.' It was to become one of many institutions, with the accumulated legacies of two thousand years being cast away as things of little worth.

A quick glance at available statistics, over those years, shows a startling falling off in all the relative departments of Church life. Vocations, baptisms, conversions, and church marriages, took a downward plunge. The only increase was in the number of those who walked out of the Church.

Many preferred to read the liturgy of the Mass in their homes, on Sundays and days of obligation, rather than see its once dignified movements parodied, and hear the historic language cheapened, in church.

In England, between the years 1968 and 1974, it has been reckoned that some two and a half million people fell away; and, if one may add to that the selling of Catholic journals, the most popular of these, *The Universe,* had an average weekly circulation of nearly three hundred and twelve thousand in 1963. Nine years later that figure had dropped to under a hundred and eighty thousand.

In France, with eighty-six per cent of the population officially Catholic, ten per cent put in an appearance at Mass; while a similar figure from 1971 to 1976, applied even to Rome. During the same period, in South America, once regarded as one of the toughest nuts for anti-clericals to crack, and where the people were commonly regarded as being steeped in superstition, an estimated twenty-five thousand priests renounced their vows. Vatican sources reported that there were three thousand resignations a year from the priesthood, and that figure took no account of those who dropped out without troubling to get ecclesiastical approval.

The Catholic part of Holland, where the new teaching was paramount, was in a truly parlous condition. Not a single candidate applied for admission to the priesthood in 1970, and within twelve months every seminary there was closed. In the

United States, in the seven years prior to 1974, one in every four of the seminaries put up their shutters.

The traffic was all one way, for apart from the recorded drop in church attendance, a regular procession of priests and nuns, in the spirit of the new freedom, were deciding that marriage offered a more comfortable daily round than life in the presbytery or cloister. 'Rebel priest, aged fifty, weds girl of twenty-five'-so ran a typical headline in the Daily *Express* of 9th September, 1973. The marriage was celebrated in a Protestant church, where the attendance was brightened by priests and nuns who were all professionally geared to add their blessings to the confetti.

Many priests had passed beyond the hinting stage and were now openly declaring in favour of abortion. As for the Sacrament of Matrimony, as more and more couples tired of encountering the same face at breakfast, the Church discovered that it had been wrong in pronouncing them man and wife. Pleas of consanguinity, non-consummation, or that neither party had been validly baptised, were the order of the day, and the granting of annulments became quite a flourishing business.

By 1972, a few years after the rot had set in, Pope Paul personally disposed of some four thousand cases. Thus encouraged, a veritable flood of applications followed. Very few of those in search of 'freedom' were definitely refused, but were advised to try again or to come back later. In Trenton, New Jersey, Bishop Reiss was so overworked that he nominated seventeen extra priests to help him (I quote his own words) 'beef up' the number of annulments.

2.

In March 1981 the Vatican took the quite superfluous step, so it seemed to many, of reiterating its Canon Law 2335, which stated that any Catholic who joined a secret society faced excommunication. To the man in the street, who was unaware that dozens of clerics, some in the highest offices of the Church, had already broken that law, it seemed a mere formality. But the Vatican, acting on information received, knew very well what it was doing. It was protecting itself, in advance, from any likely effects of a scandal that broke in May of the same year.

The Government of the country, headed by Christian Democrats, was formed of a coalition that included Socialists, Social Democrats, and Republicans. But the Communists were now demanding a place in the coalition, for political ends that left no doubt of their intentions. 'The problem is,' they said, 'to remove democratic institutions, the State apparatus, and economic life from the Christian Democratic power structure.'

But their efforts failed. The Christian Democrats held firm. So their enemies resorted to a weapon that has proved no less deadly in political warfare than assassination. They brought about a far reaching scandal which, they hoped, would topple the existing order of government in Italy.

It was made to appear, as part of the repercussions which, following the break-up of Michele Sindona's financial empire, had rumbled through the early summer of 1981, that the activities of a widespread and dangerous secret society, known as Propaganda Two (P2 for short) had come to light. But in the confused world of politics and finance things do not happen as simply as that. The people who, when compelled to do so, cry out against the machinations most loudly, have invariably been part of the backstairs conspiracy. The fact of frauds being brought into the open may be through personal spite, disappointed blackmail, or the probing of some over-zealous underling — 'why couldn't he keep quiet?' And the self-righteous profiteers who, from their lofty moral pedestals but with their pockets suffering, cannot do less than publicise the swindle, have to fume in private.

The exposure of P2 began when the police received a mysterious call advising them to search the home of Licio Gelli, a prestigious name in secret societies, and to investigate his relationship with the erstwhile barrow-trundler Michele Sindona.

The mere mention of Sindona made the implicated members of the Curia think of how to avoid being caught up in the scandal. Hence their apparently unnecessary reminder to the world at large that Canon 2335 was still valid. Meanwhile the police had come upon a suitcase in Gelli's house containing the names of nine hundred and thirty-five members of P2.

There were many prominent politicians, including three Cabinet ministers and three under-secretaries; army generals and navy chiefs; leading bankers and industrialists, secret service heads, diplomats, judges, and magistrates; civil servants in foreign affairs, defence, justice, finance, and the treasury; top names in radio and television, and the managing director, editor and publisher of Italy's leading newspaper, *Corriere Della Sera*.

Many others resigned, while a whole host of others came crashing down, like so many Humpty Dumpties, when the lists were published. More sizeable litter followed as the government of Arnaldo Forlani, in its entirety, was swept off the wall. The accusers and their victims were, of course, all members of the same gang. It was a case of 'Brothers falling out' with a vengeance. The usual accusations and recriminations followed, involving every degree of crime, even murder. The falsification of accounts, espionage, and official stealing, passed as minor considerations.

Through it all the Vatican reacted with only a mild fluttering of hearts. For although the Church had shed its aura of reverence, and its prestige had been reduced to a shadow, it remained inscrutable. The ghost of its former self was still potent. The fatally loaded guns might be levelled against its walls, but there was no cannoneer to apply the match.

It was a wise cynic who said: 'In Italy religion is a mask.'

3.

Although no churchman had been named in the scandal, the breaking of the Sindona story indirectly led to the Church reviewing its attitude to the secret societies. This had, according to orthodox belief, been settled by the said Canon Law 2335, which forbade any Catholic, on pain of excommunication, to join one. But in spite of that, because so many clerics, including members of the Curia, had broken that law, negotiations between the two sides, started in 1961, had been carried on for eleven years, with Cardinal Bea, the Pope's Secretary of State (whose name was as doubtful as his nationality), assisted by Cardinal Konig of Vienna, and Monsignor J. de Toth, putting forward a more amenable version of the Church's viewpoint.

These prolonged talks were more concerned with ironing out past differences than with formulating any future policy. But they managed to keep off the subject of hidden designs against the Church, which had partly prompted the latter's ban. Then came further discussions at Augsburg in May, 1969, where consideration was given to Papal pronouncements that roundly condemned the societies; and there was more apprehension in conservative quarters when such equivocal terms as placing Papal Bulls in their 'historical context,' and the removal of past injustices, were used to explain the purpose of the assemblies.

The outcome of this newly founded relationship fully justified the doubts of those who feared that the Church was giving ground, and going back on its judgments that had been defined as final; and that the thin end of the wedge was being imposed became apparent in July of the same year, after a meeting at the monastery of Einsiedeln, Switzerland.

It was there confidently anticipated, by Professor Schwarzbaver, that no reference to the seamy side of secret societies would be made. Neither was it. Instead it was announced that Rome's previous rulings on relationship between the Church and secret societies had not been contained in Papal Bulls or Encyclicals but in Canon Law which, as every 'updated' cleric knew, was being revised.

This occasioned more serious doubt in orthodox quarters. It was recalled that Canon Law refers to a body of laws, authorised by the Church, and 'binding to those who are subject to it by baptism.' Could it mean that such terms as binding, revision, and alterations, were on the point of being subjected to new interpretations? Moreover, more than one Papal Bull had certainly contained a condemnation of the societies.

The societies (and this must be repeated) had no intention of refuting their original intention of undermining the Church. They had no need. They had so far succeeded in their design. Their own men had infiltrated and taken over the Church at every level; and to such an extent that the Church seemed in a hurry to abandon what was left of its original claims, its historic rites, and majesty; and now the societies waited for their picked men, Cardinals and others, to present themselves before the world, cap in hand, and cry aloud their past errors of judgments.

A definite move towards this came from the once highly orthodox centre of Spain, where Father Ferrer Benimeli put forward the extraordinary plea that Papal Bulls, condemning the societies, could no longer be regarded as valid.

An undertaking that strictures imposed by Canon Law on secret societies in the past would not again be invoked, was given by Cardinal Konig when Church and secular representatives met at Lichtenau Castle in 1970. Then came the statement that Canon Law and Papal Bulls had been all very well in the twelfth and thirteenth centuries, but such documents now had a mainly historical significance, and their import could not be enacted by a Church that was preaching the more significant doctrine of 'brotherly love' which, together with friendship and morality, 'provided one of the most excellent tenets of the societies.'

The critics of these 'get together' tactics saw in this a concession to the fraternal spirit inspired by the societies, and also a virtual endorsement of the Cult of Man that Pope Paul had preached in the United States, and in which he had been confirmed by the Masters of Wisdom.

The general result of these contacts, on the Church side, was submitted for examination by the Congregation for the Faith; and the outcome was decided in advance by the remarks and reservations that accompanied them. It was no use looking back at what the Church had formerly decided. Comparison showed that its past attitude was old-fashioned, and properly belonged to a time when it had taught 'no salvation outside the Church.'

That slogan too was outmoded; and the world's Press, including most Catholic organs, again went to work with a will as it always. did when it came to propagating views that undermined tradition and reinforced the designs of those secret society members who wore mitres in the Vatican.

With the Holy Office continuing to bend over backwards to confirm the changes, the process of secularisation gained momentum from the autumn of 1974 onwards. It was made clear that the bar against secret societies had become a dead letter, and that its abrogation was bringing relief 'to a number of good people who joined them merely for business or social reasons.' They no longer presented a danger to the Church.

The dismay occasioned by this in some quarters was summed up by Father Pedro Arrupe, General of the Society of Jesus (Jesuits), who saw it as a concession to organized 'naturalism' which, he said, had entered into the very territory of God and was influencing the minds of priests and religious. Naturalism, by dogmatically asserting that human nature and human reason alone must be supreme in all things, was another echo of the Cult of Man.

The Church's changing attitude towards secret societies was reflected in this country by John Cannel Heenan, who was appointed Archbishop of Westminster in 1963 and created Cardinal two years later. In keeping with his hopeful expectation that the Church's ban on the societies would soon be abolished, some of his senior clergy were authorised to negotiate with them. The Cardinal was then informed that a publication repeating the differences between the two sides was on sale in Catholic bookshops in his diocese.

He expressed his concern. 'If, as I suspect, it is misleading, I shall see that it is withdrawn.'

He did so, and that publication, together with all similar ones, disappeared.

An interested inquirer who wrote to the Cardinal on the matter received, in reply, an assurance that the Cardinal conveyed his blessing. The same inquirer, on calling at the Catholic Truth Society bookshop, near Westminster Cathedral, was told that there had been no dealings with the Cardinal, and that the booklets had been withdrawn 'through lack of public interest.'

The growing belief that Canon 2335 would not appear in any revised edition of Church law, together with the fact that orthodox elements were being out-manoeuvred, as they had been at Vatican II, led to the Church and the societies expressing a more open relationship.

There was, for instance, a 'dedication breakfast' at the New York Hilton Hotel in March, 1976, presided over by Cardinal Terence Cooke, seconded by Cardinal Kroll, of Philadelphia, and attended by some three thousand members of secret societies. Cardinal Brandao Vilela of San Salvador de Behia, represented Brazil.

In his speech, Cardinal Cooke referred to this 'joyous event' as marking a further stage on the road to friendship.' He regretted 'past estrangements,' and hoped that his presence there signified that the new understanding between the two sides would never again be compromised. To the Cardinals and the Masters it was not so much an outsize breakfast party as a momentous union, effected by opponents who had never before at any time come (openly) together.

Cardinal Kroll, as President of the United States Bishops' Conference, had previously been approached by Cardinal Seper,

Prefect of the Congregation for the Doctrine of the Faith, who voiced the fears of those who regretted the signs of vital changes in the Church. Seper was informed that no alteration had been made, and that none was pending within the area of central legislation.

It is still, and in all cases,' said Kroll, in a statement that even to read causes a raising of the eyebrows, 'forbidden for clerics, religious, and members of secular institutes to belong to a secret society organization...... Those who enrol their names in associations of the same kind which plot against the Church, or the legitimate civil authorities, by this very fact incur excommunication, absolution from which is reserved for the Holy See.'

It was true that no active plot against the Church was then in motion. The societies could well afford to sit back and to take breath; not through any decisive change of heart, but because the first stage of the plot had been successfully accomplished. Two of the societies' choosing, in the persons of John XXIII and Paul VI, had occupied Peter's Chair. Others of their kind, who had received a red hat or a Bishop's mitre, had dominated their counsels. The next move in the plot against the Church was being reserved for the future, when the innovations in doctrine and practice had been accepted by a generation who had never known what it was to respond to the guiding hands of Popes such as the now belittled Pius XII.

The rearguard, for so the anti-Liberals may be called, made what capital it could by harking back to Canon 2335, and to the Sindona scandal as illustrating the widespread disasters brought about by contact with a secret society. As part of this campaign, a German Episcopal Conference of Bishops was held in the middle of 1981, where it was stressed, without any qualification, that 'simultaneous membership of the Catholic Church and of a secret society is impossible.'[25]

---

[25] The full text is given in *Amtsblatt des Ezzbistums*, Cologne, June 1981 issue.

This was followed by the Italian Government approving a Bill to outlaw and dissolve all secret societies, and reminding Catholics that excommunication was still the Church's penalty for joining one.

But both the German and Italian pronouncements were merely smoke screens; and none recognised this more than the societies, who were not in the least impressed. That Canon 2335, if it appeared at all in any revised edition of Church law, would be shorn of its urgency, had passed from being rumour and newspaper gossip to becoming an imminent fact. An English prelate, Cardinal Heenan, had said more than that, and had even anticipated it being abolished. While a leading official of the societies in Rome, unruffled, said he had it on good authority that Canon Law was being revised, as it was, in fact, by a Commission of Cardinals that had been set up by John XXIII and continued under Paul VI.

The official went on to say that the still apparent differences between the Church and the societies were all part of the conflict in the Vatican between the traditionalists and the progressives. 'This may well have been' — and he could well afford to shrug it off their last attack upon us.'

That pronouncement, like every other emanating from the same quarter, has proved to be correct.

For it has now to be accepted, according to a statement from the Holy See, that 'The Sacred Congregation for the Doctrine of the Faith has ruled that Canon 2335 no longer automatically bars a Catholic from membership of Masonic groups.'

4.

It had probably been by Pope Paul's own wish, in defiance of a custom that was part of a Christian's, and especially a Catholic's, second nature, that, after his death in 1978, there was no crucifix, nor even the most common religious symbol, a cross, on the catafalque when his body was placed for veneration in St. Peter's piazza.

Was it a silent acknowledgment that his work, in compliance with the secret counsel enjoined upon him since the time he became Archbishop of Milan, had been well and truly done?

Part Eleven

O VILLAIN! thou hast stolen both mine office and my name.

Shakespeare.

To those unacquainted with the power and scope of secret societies, the personality of Pope Paul VI presents a veritable enigma. No other Pope, even in the most tempestuous times, has been the subject of such conflicting reports; no other Pope has been so apparently self-contradictory.

Even a casual reading of his reign leaves an impression of doubt, equivocation, and a pathetically weak kind of hedging that is a far remove from the assertive Pontificates of the past.

For how can one account for a Pope lamenting, as Paul did, that one can no longer trust the Church? He signed the documents that kept Vatican Two on course, and promised, almost in the early hours of his reign, to consolidate and implement its decisions. Yet he changed his tune even before the last of its sessions. One would have believed the Council would have brought sunny days for the Church's history. On the contrary, they are days of storm, cloud, and fog. How did this come about?'

And the answer he provided: 'We think there has been the influence of a hostile Power. His name is the Devil'-tempts one to ask whether that was a form of confession, a self-indictment.

Was he merely expressing what he knew had become fact, or speaking as a victim, a disillusioned man in the grip of forces beyond his control?

Compare his judgments with those of almost any of his predecessors, a Pius V, a Leo XIII, and the contrast appears to be, as I said before, quite pitiful. To quote but two instances. On September, 1972; he came down heavily against the suggestion that women might play some part in the ministry of the priesthood. Such a departure from custom was unthinkable. Yet his was not a decisive voice, for only some three weeks later the Vatican issued a hand-out to journalists announcing that the Pope might change his mind. The final contradiction came on 29 March, 1973, when the Associated Press reported: 'Pope Paul ruled today that women, regardless of whether they are nuns, may distribute Communion in Roman Catholic churches.'

The Pope had already, in May 1969, condemned a new departure that had crept in whereby Communion was received in the hand. Yet later he took that stricture back, with the meaningless proviso that Communion bread could be so received after proper instruction.'

His weakness, his yielding to innovation in ritual and practice, together with the acceptance of revolutionary Marxism, and the many strange rumours that issued, from time to time, from the Vatican, caused many people in more than one part of the world to wonder if they were indeed witnessing the fall of Rome.

It was said that the Pope's correspondence, before it reached him, passed through the hands of Casaroli, Villot, and Benelli, the Cardinals in virtual control of the Vatican. Statesmen and churchmen who paid official visits found Pope Paul diffident, almost vague, and more ready with comments and opinions than with definite answers. He lacked clarity; and as wonder gave way to a feeling of disquiet various theories emerged to account for the air of mystery around Peter's Chair.

The most feasible one, that Paul was an anti-pope, a trained Communist infiltrator, could be supported by his known past, his friendship with the anarchist Alinsky and others of his kind in Milan, and the heresies he had fostered since coming to power.

Other explanations will be advanced here (not because they figure among the beliefs of the present writer, who regards them as extravagant, some wildly so), but in order to make known what many intelligent people have come to think in the face of a situation akin to those, in centuries past, when the forces of St. Michael and Asmodeus clashed by the banks of the Tiber.

One theory is that Paul VI, a good Pope in the normal sense, fell into the hands of agents of secret societies (and here the names of Villot, Casaroli, and Benelli crop up again), who drugged him, injected poison into his veins, and made him incapable of reasoning, so that all that purported to be stamped by the magisterium of the Church came, in reality, from the triumvirate of Cardinals.

But that would seem to be ruled out by Montini's life-long attachment to Marxism, which would have obviated the need for the Left orientated secret societies to exert any pressure upon him.

That would have been superfluous. Though there was one utterance by the Pope, when a dignitary asked him to quieten the widespread alarm, that might have been taken as indicative:

'Do you people believe the Pope to be badly informed, or subject to pressure?'

At length stories emanating from Rome of sacrilege and abuses committed in church, with the approval of the Pope, became so startling, that groups of people in Europe and America decided to take action.

This culminated in a Mr. Daniel Scallen of the Marian Press in Georgetown, Ontario, Canada, employing the Pinkerton Detective Agency in New York to investigate. One of the agency's detectives was sent, in 1973, to Rome, and he returned with a story that dwarfed all other speculations, however sensational.

He had determined that there were two Popes living in the Vatican, Paul VI and an impostor who had been made to resemble Montini with the aid of plastic surgery. Several such operations were necessary, and when colour photographs of the false Pope were sent to interested circles in Munich, where the imposture is still receiving concentrated study, there were certain noticeable differences in the two sets of features that could not be overcome.

To point out the differences: Montini had clear blue eyes, large, and being long-sighted he only required glasses for near viewing. The impostor had green eyes, small, and he wore glasses with thick lenses on all occasions.

Montini's photographs reveal a small mole, or birth-mark, between the left eye and the left ear.

This does not appear in photographs of the impostor, whose left eyebrow was nearer to the eye than was Montini's.

The differences between the nose and the ears of the two men are held to be decisive. Montini's nose was Roman, and protruded somewhat over his mouth. The impostor's nose, part straight and part hooked, was short, and those who subjected the photographs to professional examination claim to have detected the insertion of a plastic strip in the nose to make it appear more straight.

But it is differences in the shape and formation of the ears that present the greatest difficulty to those who doubt the existence of an impostor. Such differences are unique, individual, and they are treated the same as finger-prints in courts of law. Any comparison of the lobes and build of the ears, as revealed by photographs, becomes not a little impressive.

But the interested circles did not stop there. They turned their attention upon the voice, and called in the help of the Type B-65 Kay Elemetrics of Pine Brook, New Jersey, and the Ball Telephone Company. Their object was to analyse the voice (or voices, if there were indeed two popes) when they pronounced the traditional Easter Sunday and Christmas Day blessing, with the words *Indulgentium Peccatorum*, spoken from the Vatican in 1975.

On both occasions the message was broadcast over Rome, and many people taped it; and it appeared, according to sonograms that were made-and sonograms are more sensitive than the ear-that the man who had spoken at Easter, and again at Christmas, had not been one and the same.

There had been two different speakers.

Here I quote from those who are qualified to judge the sonograms and sum up the distinctions: One voice had a much lower pitch than the other, with a more pronounced dragging of word syllables.

Another difference was that one voice had a much lower range of frequencies. It emitted a more hissing sound, and was noticeably shaky.

These graphs were submitted to the F.B.I. for examination, and the same conclusions were arrived at. The voice patterns were different, and indicated that the vocal chords, the mouth, and the lips, were unique to each individual.

Subsequent statements alleging that there was a false Pope Paul VI, go on to say that he was an actor whose initials are P.A. R., and that it was he who died at Castelgandolfo on 6 August, 1978. A German Bishop, who claims to have proof that Montini was last known to be living not in the Vatican but in the outskirts of Rome, hopes to make this public in a forthcoming book.

So could this point to the fact that the genuine Paul VI was held captive in the Vatican, or that he was kidnapped, perhaps murdered? A layman in search of more concrete evidence went to Brescia, where some of Montini's relations were living. There a niece informed him that they were perfectly well aware of the imposture, but that all their efforts to make it known had been stifled.

The investigator, who was obviously untried and filled with a crusading zeal to bring things into the open, soon landed in trouble. He was jailed for four years, and afterwards deported from Italy.

All efforts to trace his whereabouts since then have failed.

Well, as part of the prevailing confusion in the Roman stronghold, that is what some far from negligible people have come to believe.

Part Twelve

No Roman was ever able to say: 'I dined last night with the Borgias.'

Maz Beerbohm.

A disillusioned priest who, nonetheless, still says Mass daily and fulfils all the duties demanded by a parish, merely shrugged his shoulders when I mentioned the possibility of crimes being perpetrated in the Vatican today.

'Well,' he said, 'such things have always happened there. Why shouldn't they still be going on?'

He was not in the least troubled by my suggestion. An enemy of Rome could not have been more casual, more resigned to the use of poison and the strangler's cord, and the acceptance of adultery, in high places.

The two complaints of malaria and gout figure among the causes of death of quite a few Popes.

But sometimes they could be contracted into a single word, poison, as in the case of Gregory V who reigned from 996 to 999. The same could be said regarding the death of Damasus II who, after being elected on July 17, 1048, lived for only three weeks.

Celestine II, a one-time disciple of Abelard, was made Pope on September 26, 1143, and died in the second week of the following March. There were those about him who more than suspected poison. In June 1517 the Medici Pope Leo X narrowly escaped a plot led by Cardinal Petrucci, and four other Princes of the Church, to poison him. Leo XI died on April 27, 1605, after a reign of only twenty-seven days. His death, according to official biographers, was caused by a sudden chill aggravated by the cares of office. But there were those on hand who had seen him droop over a poison cup.

Between those two short-lived pontificates, the Vice-Chancellor of the Roman Church, Rodrigo de Borgia, who was to stamp the period and his family with an infamy that was rare at any time, took his seat on the Papal throne in 1492 as Alexander VI.

As well as several secondary ones, he had already taken as his principal mistress a married Roman lady, Vanozza de Cataneis, who presented him with three sons and a daughter, all of whom lived under their father's wing as favoured members of the Court; and from the first, apart from the gestures and protestations that were inescapable parts of his office, the mainspring of Alexander's life became the advancement and political security of his family.

The oldest son, Juan, Duke of Gandia, rivalled his father in the number of illicit relationships in which he figured. His brother, Caesar, not a whit behind him in this, was to add his own distinctive brand of crime to the Borgia annals. When he was only seventeen Alexander created him Cardinal, though Caesar was never more than a sub-deacon, certainly not a priest. His papa was equally obliging when Caesar, although a Prince of the Church (he soon dropped the sham) wanted to marry. The necessary dispensation was soon forthcoming.

The youngest of Alexander's sons, Jofre, married an illegitimate daughter of Alonso II of Naples.

Then came Lucrezia who, because of her sex and the manifestly pious strain she exhibited in such surroundings, has been badly treated by novelists and historians of the Hollywood type. She was, according to the time, sufficiently ungirlish to deal with her father's official correspondence when he was out of Rome, and we know nothing definite to her discredit.

Her first marriage, to a prince of the Sforza house, was annulled on the grounds of non-consummation. Her second was to another of the illegitimate brood produced by the Neapolitan king, while her third was to Duke Alfonso d'Este of Ferrara.

Lucrezia died young, but not before she had passed through the strange experience of knowing that her second husband had been strangled by her brother Caesar. But that was not the highlight of Caesar's career, for he also dealt, in similar fashion, with his own brother Juan. He then turned his attention to Cardinals, those with money, and used his ready hands, or the always convenient poison, to account for several, including Cardinal Michele, who was a nephew of Pope Paul II, and Cardinal Orsini.

But that by no means depleted the College of Cardinals, for apart from Caesar four other members of the Borgia clan sported the red hat. Alexander turned a blind eye on Caesar's exploits, though he was genuinely grieved by the loss of his first-born, Juan.

During this time the Devil made his presence felt, sometimes visibly, in Rome, and the populace had no doubt but that the dregs of wickedness were being stirred by doings at the Vatican. For instance, a ballet was performed there on the Eve of All Saints, 1501, at which every one of the fifty dancers was a whore picked from the streets of Rome.

One of those who came to decide that the Borgias had been in the saddle all too long was Cardinal Castellisi of Corneto. So he invited father and son to a banquet, and prepared a dose of his own mixing that was guaranteed to rid Rome of them both.

They accepted the invitation, but it so happened that Alexander had made up his mind that Castellisi was a nuisance, and he came provided with some wine that had proved so efficacious in the past.

Those were not the days of mixed drinks, but the wines were somehow mixed up as they sat at table, with the result that Alexander and Caesar got a draught of their own preparation. Amid their groaning and twisting the party hurriedly broke up. Caesar recovered, but Alexander died, duly fortified by the Sacraments of the Church.

Cause of death-malaria.

His Eminence of Corneto probably enjoyed a quiet laugh. Caesar made some amends for his evil life by dying in battle. Lucrezia was caricatured in a novel by Victor Hugo, and her name was given to the title role in an opera by Donizetti. An apologist for Alexander could say no more than that during his reign Greenland accepted the Gospel.

2.

According to a recipe that was handed down and came into the hands of Garelli, who was physician to the Habsburg Emperor Charles VI (1685-1740), the Borgias obtained their poison by first killing a pig, sprinkling its abdominal organs with arsenious acid, and waiting until putrefaction set in.

This contaminated matter, when introduced into liquids, became an active, deadly, and, in the majority of cases, almost instantaneous poison.

Great precautions were taken at the Court of Alexander VI to prevent this being written down; and some of the other methods employed to administer the poison were nothing short of ingenious. A person cutting fruit could die through touching the edge of a knife that had been brushed by the preparation; while the effect of turning a key to open a door or a box might cause a minute graze of the skin through which a fatal drop imperceptibly entered the bloodstream.

Other toxicologists affirm that there was another Borgia poison, a complex mixture consisting of a gritty and whitish powder that resembled sugar. It was known as canterella or cantoreli.

Part Thirteen

Who shall decide when doctors disagree?

Alexander Pope.

The figure of John Paul I, who succeeded Paul VI, adds yet another, and one of the most profound, to a situation that is already crowded with problems. Created Bishop by John XXIII, and made a Cardinal by Paul VI (the Popes who, between them, created and implemented the revolution), his rise to the Papal throne after having been Albino Luciano, Cardinal-Patriarch of Venice, came almost as an ecclesiastical bolt from the blue.

Humbly circumstanced, he grew up in a family where opinions, quite naturally, were formed and dominated by those of the father, a committed Left-winger; and he was in his mid-sixties when, on 26 August, 1978, he emerged from the conclave at which he had been elected, with unprecedented speed, after four ballots that covered only eight hours and forty-five minutes on the first day.

An observer with an eye on the state of affairs at the Vatican might have noted that the stage was being set for yet another Renaissance drama. And such an event was indeed figured forth by the enigmas at once presented by this (apparently) by no means uncommon Pope.

Two schools of thought, in neither of which his voice had so far been definitely heard, grew up about him. One insisted that he was bent on continuing the changes set afoot by his two predecessors; that he favoured the modernist or progressive elements, and their reforms.

Support for this was given when he rejected the title of Supreme Pontiff, and elected to be installed rather than crowned. There was no crucifix on the table that served for an altar, at his inaugural Mass. Simplicity governed all, and those who echoed the ideology of Paul VI were soon claiming that the new Pope was 'their man,' especially when he was known to have opposed the Church's teaching forbidding contraception.

On the other hand, it was said. that he contemplated the annulment of some of the innovations started by Vatican Two; that he deplored the so-called 'upward' movement that was threatening the Church; and those conservatives who looked for an endorsement of their viewpoint were encouraged when the time came to appoint new Bishops to vacant sees, and, more especially, one to his old Patriarchate of Venice.

In that he was opposed by Cardinal Baggio (known as Ceba to the secret societies) whose candidate was a certain Monsignor Ce, who was known to be radical. But John Paul refused to make the appointment, thus giving support to those who wished to believe that he was in conflict with heresy.

Their satisfaction, however, was short lived, as was evidenced by an occasion when he was called upon to address a gathering of students and teachers. He led them in reciting the Angelus, but no sooner had he concluded the last 'Hail Mary' than he began to sing the praises of one whom he extolled as à classical example of abnegation and devotion to education.'

This was not, as might have been expected, a saint, nor even a simple member of the Church, but Giosue Carducci (1835-1907), who had been professor at Bologna University and whose name, as a self-confessed worshipper of Satan, was widely respected in occult circles.

His poem *Hymn to Satan*, in forty stanzas, contained such lines as the following:

'Glory to thee, magnanimous Rebel!
On Thy brow shall rise, like laurel groves,

The forests of Aspromonte.
I drink to the happy day which shall see the end
Of Rome the eternal.

To Liberty who, avenging human thought,
Overturns the false throne of Peter's successor;
In the dust with crowns and garlands!

Lie shattered, iniquitous Lord!'[26]

In shorter pieces, Carducci apologised to Satan, or the spirit of evil, which he called Agramainio, for the lies and slanders that are heaped upon him on earth. Glorifications of the occult and the Black Mass, and of Satan as the symbol of revolt against the Church, the antithesis of religion, are mixed with blasphemies. Satan is thanked for being kind, while in his *Ode to the Town of Ferrara*, Carducci cursed the 'cruel old she-wolf of the Vatican.'

Carducci became the centre of a cult, and was accorded much the same reverence by his followers that he gave to Satan. Processions were held, preceded by a banner on which Satan, in all his regalia of horns, tail, and hooves, was depicted, and at which a parody of the Litany, including the line 'Gloria in profundis Satanae' was chanted. The last eight verses of the hymn by this 'singer of Satan' passed into the repertory of songs that made the rafters ring in Italian secret society meetings.

Yet Pope John Paul's admiration for this man, his holding him up as an example for teachers and the rising generation to follow, was only one of the mysteries connected with his reign.

---

[26] Joseph Leti. *Charbonnerie et Maçonnerie dans le Réveil national italien.* Translated by L. Lachet. (Paris. Ed. polyglotte, 1925.) Quoted by Alec Mellor in *Our Separated Brethren.* (Harrap, 1964.)

2.

Over the centuries Rome, insisting on her unique historical validity, had remained stubbornly aloof from negotiations with other Churches, Protestant or Orthodox. But the Second Vatican Council had opened doors so that representatives of those Churches were now exchanging views and discussing the possibilities of unity.

One such visitor to Rome was the Russian Metropolitan Monsignor Nikodim, the Orthodox Archbishop of Leningrad. Born in 1930, and becoming the youngest Bishop of any creed in Christendom, he was reputed to exhibit a pro-Soviet and anti-West bias. In 1961 he led a deputation of Orthodox churchmen to the World Council of Churches. He was awarded the United Nations' medal for peace, and became head of the Foreign Relations Department of the Moscow Patriarchate; and after attending the installation of John Paul I, he was received in audience by the Pope on September the 5th.

The meeting occurred in the study adjoining the Pope's private library, and the opening remarks, as reported probably by Father Arrupe, Superior-General of the Jesuits, or by the liberal Cardinal Willebrands (who acted as hosts to Nikodim) followed these lines: 'Welcome, dear brother,' said the Pope, coming forward from the large oak table at which he had been working, 'so close to us, and yet so far away. What shall we discover about ourselves? When will all of us, Catholic and Orthodox, be sons of the same Church?'

Nikodim responded in the same spirit. 'I wish it could be in your reign that such a thing could happen.'

The Pope asked for news of the state of religion in Russia. 'Father Arrupe tells me that you are very hopeful about the future of the Church in your country.'

Nikodim was silent for a time. Those who had met him could imagine how, when pausing for an answer, his eyes showed as little more than slits under bushy brows. 'Most Holy Father, I'll be frank with you,' he said at length. 'In Russia they think very badly of me. They say I am working with the State authorities, and that I serve them rather than God. Yet I am a faithful servant of God.'

That short confession brought a rush of colour to his cheeks. He breathed quickly, in the grip of some violent emotion.

John Paul asked quietly: 'What do you wish me to do?'

When able to speak again, Nikodim continued: 'Most Holy Father, how can we work together if Russia still thinks that the Orthodox Church is part of the Communist system? One day I shall be crushed' — he flung out his arms — 'and the Russian Orthodox Church will come to an end. You must come to an understanding, and negotiate with them as they ask you to.'

Had that been the object of Nikodim's visit? We shall never know, for by now his physical state was truly alarming. His hand was pressed to his left side, as though, it was later said (perhaps by John Paul himself), he wished to tear out his heart and fling it at the Pope's feet. He tried to speak, but failed. His mouth twisted, and only the whites of his eyes were visible.

The Pope seized and partly supported him. 'Mercy, he is ill,' he exclaimed to Willebrands, who was still within hearing. 'Quickly, Eminence, call Doctor Fontana'-the Pope's private physician.

The Pope arranged what comfort he could for Nikodim on the floor of the study. Then he opened the window. By the time the doctor arrived the Russian was dead.

It later emerged that Nikodim had been refused permission to enter France, on his way to Rome, and that he was only able to do so when a number of French Bishops interceded on his behalf.

Then, as though to account for their opposition, the French Foreign Office let it be known that Nikodim was an accredited agent of the Soviet Secret Police.

3.

Thursday, the 28th of September, 1978, had been what passed as on ordinary day at the Vatican.

The Pope, after working in his office, had received some members of the hierarchy in private audience, and then a group of prelates from the Philippines, to whom, as representatives of the most Catholic region in south-east Asia, he extended a special welcome.

Following lunch, and the usual siesta, there was more business and discussion with several of the Cardinals. Evening prayers in his private chapel had been followed by a general good-night to members of his staff, after which he retired to his bedroom on the third floor of the Apostolic Palace.

Friday dawned as a typical end-of-September day, with the rows of Palace windows taking shape in the dull grey light and the first sounds coming, not from birds in the Vatican Gardens, but from the little room where Sister Vicenza, a nun who had been in the service of Popes for the past ten years, was preparing coffee. Her timing, her movements, and the details of her task, had an almost military precision.

It had turned five o'clock. At ten minutes past she would place the cup of coffee, always strong, in the sacristy adjoining the chapel where the Pope knelt, in meditation, before saying Mass at five-thirty. She was therefore surprised when, not hearing any movement, she had gone to the sacristy and found that the coffee, half-cold in the cup, had not been touched.

One of the Papal secretaries, Don Diego, then joined her; and when five-twenty came, and still the Pope had not appeared, they went to the door of his bedroom. There the secretary tapped, more than once, and having received no answer he opened the door.

The Pope lay on his bed, fully dressed, and obviously dead. On the bedside table was a lamp, still burning, and a cheap little alarm clock that he had brought from Venice. In the corridor was a red light emanating from an electric bell. It was placed there as an alarm, to summon help, and its glow meant that such a signal had been made by the Pope who, as Diego saw at a glance, had died alone without his call being answered. He had worn the Fisher-man's Ring for only thirty-three days.

The Pope's other secretary, Father John Magee, was next on the scene, and as the news spread Cardinal Confaloniere, Dean of the Congregation of Cardinals, who arrived at the bedside, pronounced what was afterwards accepted as the regular and official version of the tragedy.

The resulting description might relate to the death-bed of any outstandingly religious man. The Pope was on the bed, supported by pillows, with his head, turned a little to the right, inclining forward over his chest. His eyes were open. The prevailing impression was one of calmness and serenity, with no suggestion of pain. There was nothing to belie the name 'smiling Pope' that had been given him during his brief time in Rome. One hand held some sheets of paper containing notes for a speech he intended to deliver on the following day. A copy of Thomas a Kempis's *Imitation of Christ* was on the floor. [*The author is here repeating the sanitized version provided by the Vatican and challenged by David Yallop in his book 'In God's Name'*]

In the near panic and stupefaction that followed, Don Diego, who might have been expected to join in, was holding a hurriedly excited conversation on the telephone. It later transpired that he had called Doctor Antonio da Ros, begging him to come at once to the Vatican to carry out an external examination of John Paul whom he had known and treated for some twenty years-an extraordinary act for a secretary to carry out on his own initiative, when he was surrounded by a bevy of influential prelates; and doubly surprising since Doctor da Ros was not in Rome, but in Venice.

The news was released through Vatican Radio at seven-thirty-one, and on Italian Radio the morning's announcer cut short the latest act of terrorism by the Red Brigade to say: 'We interrupt this broadcast to bring you grave news...'

The tolling of bells throughout the city, and the lowering of the yellow and white Vatican City flag, took up the story; and away in Cracow, when the tidings were heard in the old building that housed the cathedral Curia, a man who had been seated at breakfast suddenly rose and retired to the private chapel. Those who saw him at the time remembered how Karol Wojtyla, for that was his name, was deathly pale and trembling, as though some heavily charged mission, whose import had been made known to him by some secret counsel in the not too far off past, was on the point of reaching fulfilment.

Those who experienced it have no hesitation in saying that from then on an atmosphere, hitherto unknown there, passed into the Vatican. Men began almost to question themselves, as they did others. Small groups met, and talked without animation. They were under a nameless pressure that it was beyond the power of any among them to remove. Much of the conversation there, at normal times, is highly allusive, causing one to search into their classical, historical, or literary memories to find a reason for it, or an answer.

Now that impression was heightened, as when Cardinals Poletti and Baggio came face to face, both aware of a question, and both equally nervous lest the other might solve it. One of them took refuge in recalling the words of Antonio Fogazzaro, the anticlerical writer.

'Eminence,' said one, 'you jeer at anyone who holds his tongue. Dread his silence!' A less experienced priest came nearer to summing up the situation in more picturesque language. 'The cupboards of the Vatican are full of skeletons. Their bones are beginning to rattle.'

'What if they are?' said another cleric. 'They were placed there during the great heresies of the Middle Ages. Now those heresies have come again.'

Rumours, mystery, embarrassment, perplexity.... It came almost as a relief when movements were heard in the hall-way that led to the Pope's bedroom. The Swiss Guards, before the termination of their four hours' duty there, were marching out, and a high temporary partition was being erected round the bed. At the same time, all exits and entrances to that part of the building were sealed.

Before long the dead Pope's brother and sister, Eduardo and Amelia Luciani, and a niece Pia, had arrived. They were plain, simple people, who would be regarded, by some in Rome, as rugged sons and daughters of the mountains (they came from the Dolomites), and not the sort to impress, in spite of their closeness to the dead Pope, a Cardinal like Villot who, now in charge of Vatican affairs and worldly to a degree, covered an iron nature with a more than usual share of French courtesy.

Worried by the sudden and unexpected death of their brother, they voiced their agreement, with most of the doctors, that an autopsy must be held to settle the matter and dispel any lingering doubts.

Professor Prati, consultant of. the heart unit of St. Camillo hospital, said an autopsy was not only desirable, but necessary. Professor Alcona, head of the neurological department of the Polyclinic of the Catholic University of Rome, gave his more downright opinion that it was the *duty* of the Holy See to order a post-mortem. The same theme was to be more strongly renewed after the Pope's funeral when another specialist, Professor Fontana, said: 'If I had to certify, under the same circumstances, the death of an ordinary unimportant citizen, I would quite simply have refused to allow him to be buried.'

Many publications were equally insistent that a post-mortem was necessary, among them being the conservative group Civilta *Cristiana,* under its director Franco Antico, and the influential *Corriere della Sera,* of Milan. Their doubts were supported by the way in which the specialists, who examined the Pope's body, contradicted each other. Doctor Buzzonetti, the first doctor on the scene, said the Pope had suffered an acute coronary thrombosis. Another put it down to cancer, while a third said the Pope had an apoplectic fit resulting from a brain tumour. Doctor Rulli of the St. Camillo hospital, said it was a case of cerebral haemorrhage.

The suggestion of heart trouble was discountenanced by Edouardo and Amelia Luciani, while Monsignor Senigallia said that John Paul, acting on his advice, had had an electrocardiogram which lasted for twenty minutes, and that no irregularity had been revealed.

The official investigators now adopted a new line to help them out of an embarrassing situation. They suddenly announced that the Pope had, from the first, been a very sick person; that he had been baptised soon after birth since he had not been expected to live through the day; that he had been in hospital eight times, in a sanatorium twice, and had undergone four operations. Appendicitis, heart, and sinus trouble, with swelling of the hands and feet, were also numbered among his complaints. His fingernails had turned black, he had managed to survive with a single lung, while there was also talk of an embolism, or blood clot.

If this summary of ills had been true (and he underwent the usual medical examination before the conclave) he would not have been elected. Within a few hours, when the initial feeling of shock had been passed, a veritable campaign of suspicion made itself felt, from which only Villot, and a few of his close associates stayed aloof. There was talk of a more than medicinal dose of digitalis, of the rare wickedness that would be necessary to introduce poison into the wine used for Mass, and of the unobtrusive ways in which a man might be helped to die.

But these hazards apart, with such terms as murder, assassination, and poison beginning to be heard, there were some unanswerable questions that were threatening, as one prelate put it, to shake the pillars of the Vatican to their very foundations.

The first one to look on the face of the dead Pope was Don Diego, a secretary. He must have seen something that thoroughly alarmed or shocked him, since he had rushed to the telephone to call Doctor da Ros, a more intimate medical friend of John Paul than any on the Vatican rota, although the average of fourteen prominent specialists it numbered were readily available, while da Ros was three hundred miles away.

Moreover, Don Diego was never asked to account for his action, or, at least, not in a way that was ever the subject of any known inquiry. And, normally loquacious, he became reserved, and could never be drawn to enlarge upon the reason why, with so much threatening to break about him, he rushed to the telephone to make a distant call.

What had he seen? Had it been the expression on the face of John Paul? According to the octogenarian Dean of the Congregation of Cardinals, Confalonieri, the dead man appeared serene, smooth, peaceful, with a hint of smiling. But a young cleric who had recently been accredited to the Vatican, and who pressed forward with a beginner's eagerness and ardour to make himself familiar with its affairs, saw a very different countenance from the one officially described.

It was distorted by a pronounced look of suffering, while the mouth, instead of presaging a smile, was gaping wide. That this latter version was true was borne out when the embalmers arrived, the four brothers Signoracci from the Medical Institute.

Their combined and highly practised efforts, carried out for two hours on the face alone, and with the aid of cosmetics, could not overcome, still less remove, the manifestation of horror that the dead Pope carried to his tomb.

But the greatest obstacle, in the way of a comfortable explanation, was the red light in the corridor. It was controlled by an electric bell on the Pope's bedside table, and it was a signal that meant he was calling for assistance. That signal had certainly been made. The red glow had sprung into life. But it had not been answered. Not by any of the guards, nor by any of the staff, the secretaries, clerks, nurse, the chauffeur, who were in the annexe; not by either of the seven nuns of the Order of Marie-Enfant who, being responsible for the Pope's domestic arrangements, were on the floor above his own.

What had they all been doing at the time? What more important task than the Pope's welfare, his safety even, had kept them employed? The police who patrolled St. Peter's Square, all through the night, must instinctively have glanced more than once at the slightly parted curtains in the Pope's bedroom. The red glow might have appeared between them. But was it indeed observable all through the night, or had it been tampered with so that it only became visible at early dawn?

There was no inquiry along those lines. Those questions went unanswered. The Pope was dead. But a post-mortem, demanded by most of the Pope's doctors and his relatives, and seconded by an influential Press, would settle all doubts as well as determining the cause of death.

But here again the tall imposing presence of Villot intervened. An autopsy, he declared, was out of the question; and his reason for saying so left the doctors more bewildered than before.

The body had been found at five-thirty a.m. Time, that is normally so regular and methodically paced at the Vatican, had then taken a surprising leap forward. For the embalmers, with quite unnecessary and unprecedented haste, had immediately been summoned, and their process had been completed by nine-thirty.

'But the intestines?' asked one of the doctors, who had made up his mind to remove them and carry out tests for a trace of poison. Villot's answer was again decisive. They had been burnt.

One of the most salient comments on the strange affair came, surprisingly enough, from *L'Osservatore Romano*, which asked whether the death of John Paul might in any way be linked to the homily he had pronounced in favour of the Satanist and devil worshipper Carducci. But only Catholics in Germany read this, for it was deleted from every copy of the paper that went elsewhere. An effort was actually made to suppress the German edition, but it was too late.

An unimpressive Press conference, that Villot could not actually oppose, though his obvious displeasure almost had the effect of a positive ban (especially when one of those present voiced the widespread regret at the failure to hold an autopsy), yielded nothing. Villot referred objectors to the final verdict given by

Father Romeo Panciroli who, after carrying out whatever check was possible on the highly-spiced and eviscerated body, was 'pleased to report that everything had been in order.'

Meanwhile a medical man, Gerin, who rejected the possibility of the Pope's death having been a natural one, openly pronounced the word 'poison;' and a Bishop (one must respect his wish to remain unnamed) made up his mind to succeed where doctors, professors, and journalists, had failed. He would penetrate the veil of silence and secrecy, and establish the truth, whatever its import or what it might entail.

He worked hard and long; interviewed countless people; delved into every department, mounted stairways and passed through devious passages in the Vatican. Then, for a time, he vanished from the scene; and those who have since met him found him not only changed, as may happen after only a few months, but in every sense an entirely different man.

Hardened Romans and realists, who had expected nothing else, merely shrugged. The dome of St. Peter's is not an egg-shell, to be cracked. He was merely one more fool who had cracked his own heart against it.

Cardinal Villot, aware of the growing disquiet in the Church, promised to make a statement on recent events in the Vatican before the calling of the next conclave. He never did, but remained a man of mystery to the last, leaving no evidence as to how much he had known (there was ample suspicion to more than make up for absence of certainty), or for how much he had been responsible. The cause of Villot's own death on 9 March, 1979, occasioned the same elementary confusion that surrounded the passing of John Paul I. The Cardinal, according to an early announcement, had died of bronchial-pneumonia. A second verdict named kidney trouble; a third, hepatitis; while yet another attributed the cause to internal haemorrhage.

It appears that top-flight Catholic specialists, when called to the bedside of their most eminent patients, reveal themselves as being very indifferent diagnosticians.

4.

It was raining. From their places on the colonnade above the piazza, Simon Peter and his fellow saints looked down upon a forest of umbrellas. The dead Pope, in vestments of red, white, and gold, and with a golden mitre on his head, had been brought from the Clementine Hall in the Apostolic Palace to the square where, in a plain cypress coffin, the body rested on a red blanket fringed with ermine, for the celebration of an open air Mass. The flame of a single tall taper, placed near the coffin, flickered this way and that in the wind and drizzle, but never to the point of going out. A Monsignor, his mind heavy with a fast growing certainty, looked round at the mostly shawled heads and white faces, and thought of the terrible suspicion that was trembling on everyone's lips.

'It is too much,' was all he could murmur to himself. 'It is too much.'

A chill October dusk, pierced by pin-points of light from the city, was closing down as the cortege moved into the basilica where, in the crypt, future generations will come to gaze at a tomb bearing the simple inscription JOHANNES PAULUS 1. And some, despite the blunting of time, may wonder.

Part Fourteen

Belief in the innocence of rulers depends upon the ignorance of those ruled.

Hugh Ross Williamson.

The Catholic world at large had barely recovered from the shock of John Paul's death, sudden and unexpected as it was, when another event diverted their attention from the *Sedis vacantia* (vacancy of the Apostolic See) to the puff of white smoke that, on 16 October, 1978, issued from the small bent chimney of the Sistine Chapel, and to the announcement that followed it: 'We have a new Pope.'

More than the usual excitement resulted, and there were those among the more experienced observers who noted that much of it came from the same quarters that had acclaimed John XXIII; from those who greeted the changes (or disasters, as many thought) that resulted from his reign, as long awaited and welcome signs that the Church was throwing off its iron archaic fetters.

For the new Pontiff was Karol Wojtyla, who received something like a hero's welcome because he was a Pole, from behind the Iron Curtain, where religion, especially the Christian, had had to run the gauntlet, and where now, although the era of blows and taunts was somewhat relaxed, it was still subject to a mainly wary and restricted acceptance. Wojtyla was, incidentally, the first non-Italian to be elected Pope since 1522.

A veteran American journalist who had the not inappropriate name of Avro Manhattan, who knew the Vatican more intimately than he did the White House, and who was well versed in Russian tergiversation, had earlier written: 'The proportion of radical Cardinals, and of future members of the Sacred College, whose political leanings range from light pink to scarlet red, has been mounting and will continue to increase. The inevitable result will be that, thanks to the greatest number of Leftist clerics, the election of a Red Pope is becoming more likely.[27]

Had such a Pontiff arrived in the person of Karol Wojtyla?

In view of the strained relationship between countries in the West, and those behind the Iron Curtain, the officially irreligious policy of the latter, and the emergence of John Paul II, as the new Pope elected to be called, a number of questions presented themselves that called for an answer. His orthodox early training and development, his becoming a priest, and his rise to Archbishop and then to Cardinal, had proceeded normally.

Many hundreds of his co-religionists in Poland during the thirty years of Communist domination, had undergone petty or serious persecution, many being jailed, some put to death. Yet there is no indication of Wojtyla ever undergoing more than the usual trials that have to be endured by known dissidents. He had not been subject to any sustained or menacing outcry, and his relationship with the Marxist authorities had been the same as that of any ordinary citizen who wore his faith upon his sleeve.

Through it all he must have been called upon, as a prelate, to give not only religious but also social, and even economic advice to those of his faith, advice that must have sometimes conflicted with the governing code. Yet he was never actually silenced, and he was tolerated, even privileged by the authorities, while his religious superior, Cardinal Wyszynski, then Primate of Poland, lived under constant pressure.

---

[27] The Vatican-Moscow Alliance, 1977.

A case in point was the granting of permission to leave the country. When the Synod of Bishops was called for Rome, both Cardinals applied for exit visas. The Primate encountered a blunt refusal, but Wojtyla was given permission as a matter of course.

He experienced the same favour when it came to attending the conclave at which he was elected, and those who had been dismayed by the prospect of a Pope from a Soviet background soon felt they were justified.

Pierre Bourgreignon, writing in *Didasco*, a French publication that appeared in Brussels, April 1979, said: 'No one capable of coherent thought will easily believe that a Cardinal from behind the Iron Curtain can be anything but a Communist plant.'

A similar doubt was expressed in *The War is Now*, an Australian production issued on behalf of Catholic tradition. If Wojtyla, it asked, is a true Catholic Pole, 'why would proper, sensible, prudent Cardinals with the Church's welfare at heart, elect a target, a man whose family and people remain under the gun, a whole nation of ready-made hostages or martyrs?'

The Abbe de Nantes, leader of the Catholic Counter-Reformation of the Twentieth Century, was more downright: 'We have a Communist Pope.'

It was formerly acknowledged that differences, when they were in Poland, did exist between the two Cardinals. Wyszynski never yielded an inch when dealing with the controllers of his country.

Wojtyla was all for coming to terms and continuing 'dialogue' with them, along the lines that had been established by Paul VI; and what was more noticeable Wojtyla, apart from never actually condemning atheistic Marxism, stood in the way of those who wished to adopt a more militant attitude towards it.

Someone had noted that during the conclave in the Sistine Chapel, at which he was elected, the solemnity of the occasion, and the fact of being overlooked by Michelangelo's gigantic frescoes of the Last Judgment, did not prevent Wojtyla reading from a book that he had thought fit to take in for instruction-or for a little light relief from the gravity of choosing the Vicar of Christ? It was a book of Marxist principles.

Those who regarded him with suspicion were not reassured when he rejected the ritual of coronation and chose to be 'installed,' and when he let it be known that he rested more easily in an ordinary chair than on the Papal throne. Were Church practices, they asked, to undergo a further paring down after those that had already resulted from the Council? Their fears grew when he put aside the mantle of authoritarianism with which the Church, of which he was now the Head, had hitherto been invested. And any lingering doubts they may have had vanished when, in his inaugural speech, he undertook to fulfil the last will and testament of Paul VI, by adhering to Pope John's directives of collegiality and the liturgy of the New Mass-and that, it may be observed, in spite of the fact that he must have been aware of all the obscenities that followed it.

When making that announcement, Wojtyla stood by a makeshift altar that, like Paul VI's bier, was bereft of any religious sign in the form of a crucifix or cross.

Other indications of what might be expected of the new Pope soon followed. In his first encyclical he praised Paul VI for having revealed 'the true countenance of the Church.' He spoke in a similar vein of the Second Vatican Council which had given 'greater visibility to the Eucharistic sacrifice;' and he undertook to follow and promote the renewal of the Church 'according to the spirit of the Council.'

A later statement referred to that Council as having been 'the greatest ecclesiastical event of our century;' and it now remained to secure the acceptance of fulfilment of Vatican Two in accordance with its authentic content. In doing this we are guided by faith.... We believe that Christ, through the Holy Spirit, was with the Council Fathers, that the Church contains, within its magisterium, what the 'Spirit says to the Church, saying it at the same time in harmony with tradition and according to the demands posed by *the signs of the times*' (my emphasis).

His remark on being in harmony with tradition was flatly contradicted by his admission that 'the liturgy of the Mass is different from the one known before the Council. But' (he added significantly) 'we do not intend to speak of those differences.' It was essential to renew the Church, in structure and function, to bring it into line with the needs of the contemporary world; and from that admission it needed but a step for Wojtyla to emphasise the revolutionary principles of 1789, with the glorification of man, liberated man, as a being who is sufficient unto himself. Man was the only idol deserving the reverence of those on earth, his stature being confirmed by and classified as the Rights of Man.

That somewhat hazy terrestrial belief has been the inspiration of every Left-wing movement from then on. With a fine disregard for the authority of law it was proclaimed, in America, that 'liberty is the very foundation of political order.' While a few years ago François Mitterrand, the Communist who is now President of the French Republic, said that 'Man is the future of Man.' It was then left for Karol Wojtyla, as John Paul II, to enshrine that belief in a modern religious setting by declaring that 'Man is the primary issue of the Church;' a Papal announcement that is thoroughly in line with the Marxist principle that 'Man is an end in himself and the explanation of all things.'

The Pope then proceeded to pass from verbal to more active approval of the political system from which he had emerged. Speaking of the Church in Poland, he said that its relationship with Communism could be one of the elements in the ethical and international order in Europe and the modern world.' He maintained a friendly understanding with the Red occupiers of his country, and thought it possible to open up a spiritual *detente* with them. In furtherance of this the Communist Minister of State, Jablonski, with a train of comrades as large as that of any Eastern potentate, was received at the Vatican. Then came the Soviet Minister, Gromyko, who was granted more than the prescribed time with His Holiness.

He greeted guerrillas between their bouts of 'freedom fighting' in Africa and Nicaragua. His moral support went with them. He opened the door of his study to the Mexican Jose Alvarez, who travelled far and wide in South America calling on extremists to light the flames of anarchy. Not even the Pope's intimates knew what passed between them. He was the star' speaker at a Latin

American Congress in Panama City, where the theme was certainly not religious, since the organisers were the Communist dictator, General Torrijos, and the Marxist Sergio Mendez Areeo, of Cuernavaca.

When addressing a group of refugees from Vietnam, Laos, and Cambodia, the Pope's lukewarm attitude was commented on by Robert Serrou, the *Paris Match* correspondent. The Pope, naturally enough, had commiserated with his audience, but why, asked Serrou, had he not so much as mentioned the Red terror from which they had escaped?

In view of that failure to condemn tyranny, it is remarkable that one of the few strictures uttered by John Paul II has been directed against those Catholics who deplore the gradual taking to pieces of the Church since Vatican Two: 'Those who remain attached to incidental aspects of the Church which were more valid in the past but have now been superseded, cannot be considered the faithful.'

His orthodoxy, when it came to the teaching of Catholicism and its relation to other religions, has also been called into question. It is a commonplace, but no belittlement of Islam, to point out that the fatalistic Arabian tradition, with its denial of Christ's divinity and of the redemption, is a far remove from the essentials of Christian belief. Yet the Pope told an audience of Moslems that their Koran and the Bible are in step.' And in more casual mood, was he pandering to the mechanical spirit of the age when he told a gathering of motorists to have the same care for their cars as they have for their souls? Or was it by a slip of the tongue that the importance attached to cars preceded that of souls?

One of the Pope's letters, dated 15 September, 1981, on the subject of private property and capitalism, shows a marked contradiction of and a departure from the Church's teaching. For in the letter he says: 'Christian tradition has never upheld the right of private property as absolute and untouchable. On the contrary, it has always understood the right as common to all to use the goods of the whole creation.'

That is so blatantly false, and so opposed to what every Pope from Leo XIII to Pius XII had said, that one is tempted to agree with those outspoken trans-Atlantic critics[28] who bluntly call Karol Wojtyla a liar, and who follow that up with the exhortation: 'Break off, Charlie!'

For here I quote from Leo XIII: 'The Socialists endeavour to destroy private property, and maintain that the individual possessions should become the common property of all, to be administered by the State or by municipal bodies.... It is unjust, because it would rob the legal possessor, bring the State into a sphere that is not its own, and cause complete confusion to the community.'

Leo went on to say that a man works in order to obtain property, and to hold it as his own private possession. 'For every man has the right by nature to possess property of his own. This is one of the distinct points between man and the animal creation.... The authority of the Divine Law adds its sanction forbidding us in the gravest terms even to covet that which is another's.'

From Pius XI: 'The primary function of private property is in order that individuals may be able to provide for their own needs and for those of their families.'

And from Pius XII: 'The Church aspires to bring it about that private ownership shall become, in accordance with the plans of the divine wisdom and with the laws of nature, an element in the social system, a necessary incentive to human enterprise, and a stimulus to nature; all this for the benefit of the temporal and spiritual ends of life, and consequently for the benefit of the freedom and dignity of man.'

And still from the same Pope: Only private ownership can provide the head of a family with the healthy freedom it requires

---

[28] The publishers of Veritas, an orthodox newsletter. Louisville, Kentucky, U.S.A.

to carry out the duties allotted to him by the Creator for the physical, spiritual, and religious well-being of his family.'

Side by side with these proclamations the Church has issued warnings against Liberalism, which ends in capitalism, and against Marxism which preaches the abolition of private property.

Therefore the statement made by John Paul II may be seen to be extraordinary compared with many of those made by his predecessors.

2.

During his early life in Cracow, both as student and as a young priest, Wojtyla acquired a liking for the theatre that has never left him. It began when he joined a school dramatic group, and later, during the war when Poland was occupied, what is often referred to as a subterranean theatre,' which means that rehearsals and performances took place in a room, sometimes the kitchen of an apartment, secretly and by candlelight.

'It was round about that time,' says one of his biographers,[29] 'that he formed a sentimental attachment to a young woman;' and from then on she has followed him like a shadow, by rumour, newspaper report, and in the conversation of Polish exiles on both sides of the Atlantic.

Sometimes the details differed. The most unlikely version, that was probably put out to engage sympathy, was that she worked against the Germans, had been discovered, and shot. Another gives the date 1940 as marking the height of their attachment. According to Blazynski, who was born in Poland, the future Pope was popular with the girls and 'had a steady girl friend.'

His love of entertainment extended to the cinema, and to such superficial mock-religious shows as Jesus *Christ Superstar*. After one performance of the latter he spoke for twenty minutes to the audience on the theme of love and joy. He encouraged the adolescent bawling and aimless strumming of guitars that, in the name of popular accompaniments, make some present day Masses unbearable to many. In the same spirit, he invited the

---

[29] George Blazynski in John Paul II (Weidenfeld and Nicolson, 1979). Some of the incidents related here are taken from that book.

American evangelist, Billy Graham, to preach one of his red-hot sermons in the church of St. Anne, Cracow.

One of the subjects discussed by the circle in which he moved was a book by the writer Zegadlowicz, which had been frowned upon by the Church because of its obsession with sex; while an early piece of writing by Wojtyla (translated by Boleslaw Taborski and quoted by Blazynski) contains such lines as 'Love carries people away like an absolute.... Sometimes human existence seems too short for love.'

The same theme occurred in Wojtyla's book *Love and Responsi*bility, 1960, which, Blazynski says, 'does not ignore the bodily reality of man and woman, and goes into considerable detail in describing both the physiology and psychology of sex (the latter often with a great deal of insight that might seem surprising in one who is now, after all, a celibate clergyman.'

Even when Wojtyla became Pope the ghost of the mystery woman who had haunted his student days was not laid. There are those among Polish exiles who claim to have known her, and one of the most downright rumours spread is that her name is Edwige.

But be that as it may, not even Wojtyla's apologists can deny that he has shown more interest in human sexuality than any Pope since the Middle Ages. Many listeners to an address he gave in Rome were quite embarrassed when he launched into details on lust and the nakedness of the body.

Some of his own statements have given publicity agents ample scope to enlarge upon them.

'Young people of France,' he cried to a far from mature audience in Paris, 'bodily union has always been the strongest language that two people can say to each other.' Those words have been called some of the most stupefying ever spoken by a Pope.

During his visit to Kisingani in Zaire, Africa, a correspondent in *Newsweek* shook his head sadly over the way in which the Head of the Roman Church dispensed with formality. In humid heat, and almost as soon as he stepped from the plane, he was seen 'grinning, sweating, swaying and stomping with dancing girls.' He has been photographed watching a group of adolescent girls in one-piece garments that reached well above the knee carry out a series of acrobatic dances. Another picture has recently come to hand in which, at Castelgandolfo, he watches a young dancer perform convolutions in front of him, with her head and face almost lost sight of in a flurry of white underclothes.

A play written by Wojtyla, *The Jeweller's Shop*, was produced at the Westminster Theatre in May, 1982. Said to be written in purple prose, the producer hoped that the play 'should draw the punters' as well as the church audiences.

His hope may well be realised since the play, still quoting *The Daily Telegraph* (28 April 1982) "embraces the unlikely subject of prostitution."[30]

---

[30] English theatre critics did not exactly acclaim the Pope's efforts as a playwright-Editor.

3.

There is no need for John Paul II to enter deeply into the differences in the Church resulting from Vatican Two. It has been said that he is walking with a rose in his hand-that is, until the early gains achieved by John XXIII and Paul VI have been consolidated. The once proud boast relating to the One True Church has diminished into a spineless acknowledgment of 'these ecumenical days.' The claim of Papal authority, which has yielded place to the idea of power-sharing with Bishops, may remain on the Church's statute books for a while longer, but the force of its divine origin has been watered down; and the altars, always a sign of 'whatever gods may be,' have been demolished.

Even so, the next phase of the attack upon the Church, from within, has passed beyond its preparatory stages and is already under way. It is likely to be less spectacular than the earlier depredations. The word 'revisionary' will be heard more often than 'change.' The churches will no longer be used as amatory playgrounds. Yet what is likely to result from meetings in the Vatican Synod Hall, between more than seventy Cardinals and Bishops, will probably, in the long run, be quite as devastating as the innovations that have now been accepted as norms by a largely unperceptive and uncritical public.

Among the subjects that are known to have been discussed are marriage and abortion; and prelates such as Cardinal Felici are rational enough to admit that the issues on these, and. similar questions, have virtually been decided in advance. Marriage annulments, robbed of much of their earlier formality, will be made easier. The threat of excommunication will be lifted from women who undergo abortion; and, a still greater earnest of more and vital concessions to come, the articles of Canon Law will be reduced from numbering 2,414 to a possible 1,728.

But these considerations will not weigh heavily on those who are likely to be impressed by the Pope's visit to this country in May this year, 1982. The power of Mr. Mark McCormack's International Management Group has been invoked to provide the same publicity for a Pope that it has so ably done for golfers, baseball toughs, and tennis players; while a firm of business consultants, Papal Visits Limited, will add further promotional backing.

The proven dramatic instinct of John Paul II will doubtless come into play as, scattering blessings from a glass-topped vehicle, he rides slowly between miles of fencing, stands, marquees, and Press platforms, and over carpet decorated with thousands of plants, to where three crosses, the tallest a hundred and twenty feet high no, Mr. McCormack, Calvary was not like that-rise above a steel and canvas altar structure.

After Mass, the faithful may come away with a screwdriver that bears a sticker showing the Pope's head on its handle. All arrangements for the visit will be in the capable hands of Archbishop Marcinkus, who has obviously been washed clean of the somewhat doubtful reputation that clung to him in Rome.

Appendix

The strange death of Roberto Calvi

Hard upon the upheaval caused by the collapse of Michele Sindona's financial empire, and the revelations concerning membership of the masonic lodge Propaganda 2, Oriental Rite, the Vatican faced a third embarrassment when on June 18, 1982, the body of banker Roberto Calvi was discovered hanging from scaffolding under Blackfriars Bridge.

Calvi had been the president of Italy's biggest private bank, the Ambrosiano, which took over many of Sindona's assets. Sometimes known as 'God's banker' because of his close connection with Vatican finance (the Vatican bank was a large shareholder in the Ambrosiano), in May of the above year he faced a number of charges related to, among others, illegal currency transactions.

He vanished from Rome and arrived in London, where he took accommodation in Chelsea Cloisters, on June 15. He was a frightened man, burdened with secrets connected with his own and the Vatican bank, into which it was not wise to probe too deeply. Some who had tried were suddenly dismissed from their posts, others went to jail on faked charges, and there had been at least one known shooting affair during investigations.

While Calvi was absent his secretary, who had been with the bank for thirty years, wrote a note cursing Calvi and then threw herself, so the authorities said, from the fourth floor of the bank's headquarters in Milan.

In London Calvi treated his chauffeur as a bodyguard. He arranged with a friend to call at his flat at regular intervals, and then to knock three times for entrance. He also shaved off his moustache, which he had worn for years.

But although disinclined to leave his apartment, Calvi, it was said, had nonetheless walked four miles in the night or early morning, to commit suicide in the unlikely area of Blackfriars.

The mention of that area calls for comment, together with a reminder that secret societies lay great stress on association and symbols. Blackfriars was the site of the friary and church of the Dominican Order, members of which acquired the name of Black Friars because of their habit. They were, and still are, known as the Order of Preachers. As such they brought the pulpit into general use, and pulpits figure in the stonework of Blackfriars Bridge. And members of the P2 lodge, in which Calvi figured as number 0519, dressed as Black Friars in white tunic, with black cloak and hood, for their ritualistic meetings.

An inquest *jury*, supported by Scotland Yard, found that Calvi had committed suicide, a verdict that caused raised eyebrows and disbelieving smiles among his relatives and the Italian Press and police. For it implied that Calvi, who was sixty-two, had displayed the dexterity of an athletic young man in seeking, as the Rome Public Prosecutor said, a complicated way to end himself.

In the dark, and on completely strange ground, he had filled his pockets with rubble, negotiated a long ladder and wet planks which had a gap of some feet between them, seized a piece of sodden rope, tied one end to his neck and the other to a piece of scaffolding, and flung himself off. Why take so much trouble, when among his belongings were found medical syringes, seven boxes of tablets, and 170 pills of various kinds, many of which could have done the trick more easily?

But here again the obscure, somewhat bizarre, yet sinister influence of P2 and other secret societies comes into the picture. The initiation of a candidate into the craft often includes the taking of an oath not to reveal any of its secrets. Should he offend, he would undergo a violent death and then be buried near water at low level within reach of the tide: the belief being that his ghost would thereby be prevented from walking, which might embarrass his murderers.

This would apply to Calvi, who in all probability had been strangled before being taken to Blackfriars, to ensure that the dangerous secrets in his possession would not be divulged. For after his mysterious and clumsy 'suicide', before his body was cut down, the Thames tide was covering his feet.

There is nothing to suggest that Calvi had offended his brother masons. But he was under legal pressure, and there were many who feared the possible bringing to light of his extensive financial network. The Vatican, ever since the Sindona scandal, had been on its guard against further revelations, and when the activities of P2 were brought into the open, it took a surprising and an apparently unnecessary step.

The Congregation for the Doctrine of Faith reminded Catholics that according to article 2335 of Canon Law they were forbidden, under pain of excommunication, to become freemasons.

This was merely a tongue-in-cheek exercise to out-step questioners since, as readers of these pages will know, some of the leading prelates at the Vatican were established masons. But the move reflected the alarm that was felt there. Two cardinals, Guerri and Caprio, had worked hand-in-glove with Sindona whose fall had brought P2 and its shady dealings into the open. A prominent member of the lodge, Umberto Ortolani, was known to have close links with the Vatican.

But the most significant name that surfaced with the scandal was that of Archbishop Marcinkus, among whose several unacknowledged connections were those with Mafia circles and with Licio Gelli, a former Grand Master of P2. But even more to the point, he was also president of the Vatican bank, the most secretive and exclusive bank in the world.

Marcinkus had also been a friend and business associate of Calvi, and having remarked that 'Calvi has our trust' he bore that out by issuing a guarantee, in the name of the Vatican bank, to cover some of Calvi's extensive loan operations, involving many millions, as part of a vast monetary programme that included international arms selling deals.

But as the storm gathered Marcinkus withdrew his guarantee, though by then sufficient evidence had come to light to justify the belief that more than normal business exchanges had passed between the Vatican bank and the Banco Ambrosiano.

The Minister for the Treasury, Andreatta, called for the Vatican to come into the open and admit its part in the crisis that was rocking the financial world. There were also demands for Marcinkus to be questioned, while pressure was put upon the Pope to dismiss him. But Marcinkus was too well versed in Vatican banking secrets for the Pope to risk his displeasure. Moreover, he had been nominated chairman of the influential Commission of Cardinals, and so was well on the way to becoming a prince of the Church, a prospect which made him unavailable for awkward contacts.

For when commissioners went to the Vatican to seek information on its bank and Calvi's relationship with it, Marcinkus was ,not at home.' And when subpoenas (implying that the recipients were subject to examination) addressed to Marcinkus and two of his clerical banking associates, were sent by registered post to the Vatican, the envelope was returned unopened.

A somewhat grudging admission that the Vatican may have been partly responsible for the Calvi bank failure was made this month (August 1982) by Cardinal Casaroli.

Meanwhile the highly controversial Archbishop Marcinkus, in his office that is just a few steps down from the Pope's apartment, may sometimes handle a balance sheet from his late colleague's bank and reflect upon the words with which such statements ended: 'Thanks be to God!'

Finale

'Ye're a bad lot; a blackguard, in the likes of a living man.'

I was thus greeted by an Irish priest early one crisp April morning. He had read in manuscript much of what I have here written, and while he could not confute it he thought that I was doing the Church a sorry service. He was a big, broad-shouldered man, with sad eyes and a knobbed stick that he swung as though it were a shillelagh.

We were standing within the shadow of St. Peter's, while the blinds were still drawn in the palace windows, and only isolated footsteps sounded on the piazza. His hint of humorous menace contrasted with the serenity of *my* feelings.

For there is nothing more golden in the world than a Roman dawn. Gold dust, lighting the past more surely than it does the present, filters through the air and settles, like a hesitant touch, on Maderna's fagade with its bold Roman letters, turning its brown and ochre tints into gold. Dust motes, where the first light catches them, are turned into gold that touches the base of Caligula's obelisk and breaks in splendour over the cobbles; over the statues of the saints on the colonnade, and the dome that gradually wears to white; over the space before the basilica surrounded by Bernini's giant columns, as once the legions surrounded the levelled spears that rose in envy of the Roman Thing; water from the fountains, whenever a breeze ruffles it, falls away in drops of gold.

The angle of the stick was inviting me to look over Vatican Hill. 'That's the way dawn will come, over the city, over the Church. Don't you believe it?'

I only half nodded.

'What you've written will pass, like a holiday or a slow fever. But the promise that was given to Peter'-and he pointed to the central figure on the colonnade-'will not pass. It cannot. The fissure in the Rock will be closed. Dawn will come again. Don't you believe it?'

'Yes,' I agreed, influenced perhaps by his sad eyes and the swing of his shillelagh. 'Dawn will come again.'

But will it be a false dawn?

Bibliography

Benson, Mgr. R. H., *Lord of the World* (Pitman, *1907*).

Blazynski, G., *Pope John Paul II* (Weidenfeld and Nicolson, *1979*).

Carpi, Pierre, *Les prophéties du Pape Jean XXIII* (Jean Claude Lattes, *1976*).

Casini, Tito, *The Last Mass of Paul VI* (Instituto Editoriale Italiano, *1971*).

Cotter, John, *A Study in Syncretism* (Canadian Intelligence Publications, Ontario, *1980*).

Cristiani, Mgr. L., *Satan in the Modern World* (Barrie and Rockliff, *1961*).

Crowley, Aleister, *Confessions* (Bantam Books, U.S.A., *1971*).

Dem, Marc, *Il faut que Rome soit détruite* (Albin Michel, Paris, *1980*).

Disraeli, Benjamin, *Lothair* (Longmans Green, *1877*).

Eppstein, John, *Has the Catholic Church gone mad?* (Stacey, *1971*).

Fahey, Fr. Denis, *The Mystical Body of Christ in the Modern World* (Regina Publications, *1972*).

Fahey, Fr. Denis, *The Mystical Body of Christ and the Reorganisation of Society* (Regina Publications, *1978*).

Gearon, Fr. P. J., *The Wheat and the Cockle* (Britons Publishing Co., *1969*).

Kolberg, Theodor, *Der Betrug des Jahrhunderts* (Munich, *1977*).

Laver, James, *The First Decadent. J. K. Huysmans* (Faber, *1964*).

Levinson, Charles, *Vodka-Cola* (Gordon and Cremonesi, U.S.A., *1979*).

Martin, Malachi, *The Final Conclave* (Melbourne House, *1978*).

Martinez, Mary, *From Rome Urgently* (Statimari, Rome, *1979*).

Mellor, Alec, *Our Separated Brethren* (Harrap, *1964*).

Miller, Fulop, *The Power and Secret of the Jesuits* (Owen, *1967*).

O'Mahoney, T. P., *The New Pope. John Paul I* (Villa Books, Dublin, *1978*).

Oram, James, *The People's Pope* (Bay Books, Sydney, *1979*).

Pinay, Maurice, *The Plot against the Church* (St. Anthony Press, *1967*).

Queensborough, Lady, *Occult Theocracy* (British-American Press, *1931*).

Rhodes, Henry, *The Satanic Mass* (Rider, *1954*).

Smith, Bernard, *The Fraudulent Gospel* (Foreign Affairs Publishing Co., *1977*).

Stoddart, Christina, *Light-Bearers of Darkness* (Boswell, *1930*).

Stoddart, Christina, *Trail of the Serpent* (Boswell, *1936*).

Symonds, John, *The Great Beast. The Life and Magic of Aleister Crowley* (Mayflower, *1973*).

Thierry, Jean Jacques, *Lettres de Rome sur le singulier trépas de Jean-Paul I* (Pierre Belfond, Paris, 1981).

Virebeau, Georges, *Prelats et Francs-magons* (Henri Coston, Paris, 1978).

Webb, James, *The Flight from Reason* (Macdonald, 1971).

Webster, Nesta, *Secret Societies and subversive movements* (Christian Book Club, http://ca.geocities.com/nt_351/webster/webster_index.html).

Williamson, Hugh Ross, *The Great Betrayal* (Tan Books, 1970).

Williamson, Hugh Ross, *The Modern Mass* (Tan Books, 1971).

Wiltgen, Fr. R. M., *The Rhine Flows into the Tiber* (Augustine Press, 1979).

Other titles

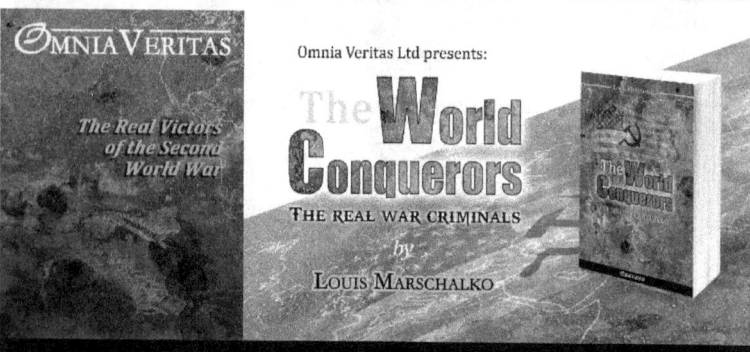
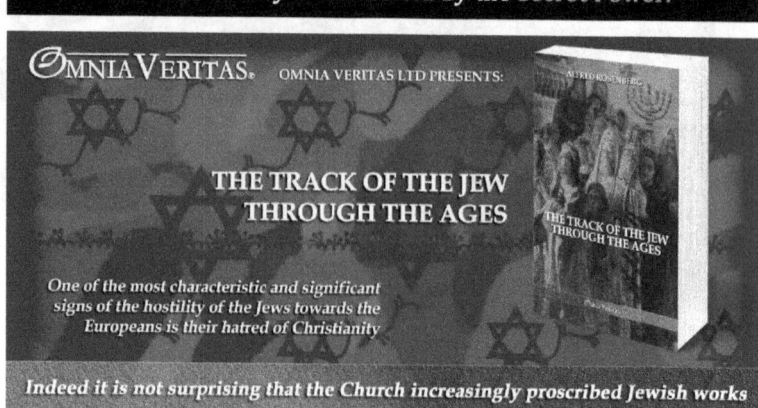

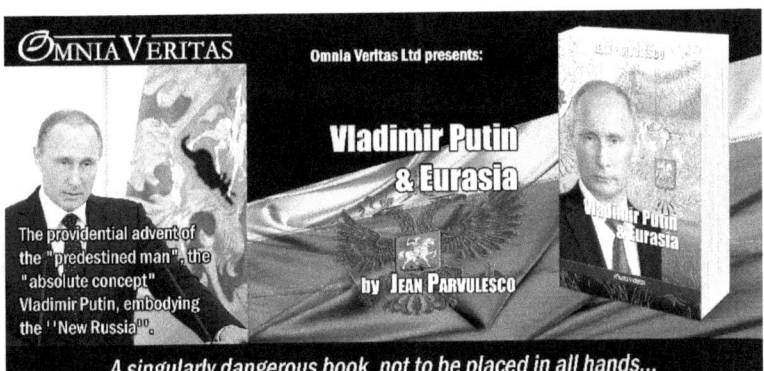

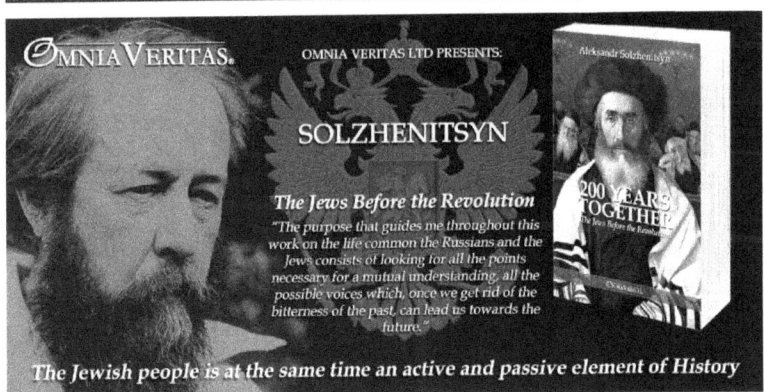

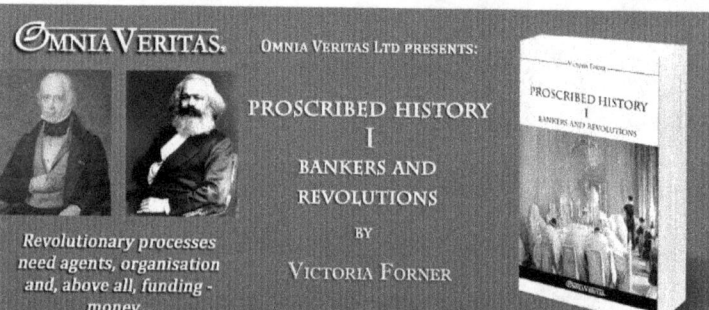

www.ingramcontent.com/pod-product-compliance
Lightning Source LLC
Chambersburg PA
CBHW050138170426
43197CB00011B/1876